UNCOVERING REASONABLE DOUBT
The Component Method

A Comprehensive Guide for the Criminal Defense Investigator

ISBN: 978-0-9670615-0-4
LOC: 98-93137
Published by: Investigative Support Specialist, Inc.
800 East Ocean Boulevard, Suite D, Stuart, Florida 34994
Call 1-800-465-5233 for additional copies.

Edited by: Dr. Richard Grego, Sr.

Special thanks to Dr. Grego for his assistance
and professional editing of the manuscript.

Design and Graphics by: Philip Galdys
Fading Image Graphics (561) 285-5072
Port St. Lucie, Florida

Printed in the United States by
Morris Publishing
3212 East Highway 30
Kearney, NE 68847
1-800-650-7888

TABLE OF CONTENTS

i Dedication
ii Acknowledgements
iv About the Author
v Foreword
vii Introduction

1-1 Chapter 1 - The Criminal Investigator's Purview
2-1 Chapter 2 - The Search For Truth:
Critical Thinking for the Criminal Defense Investigator

COMPONENT ONE
3-1 Chapter 3 - Investigative Case Review & Analysis
Investigative Outline
Investigative Journal

COMPONENT TWO
4-1 Chapter 4 - Initial Defendant Interview

COMPONENT THREE
5-1 Chapter 5 - Crime Scene Examination & Inspection

COMPONENT FOUR
6-1 Chapter 6 - The Alleged Victim & Witness Background Investigation

COMPONENT FIVE
7-1 Chapter 7 - Interviewing Witnesses

COMPONENT SIX
8-1 Chapter 8 - The Report of Investigation & Testifying

9-1 Chapter 9 - The Investigation of Domestic Violence Crimes
10-1 Chapter 10 - Crime & The Drug War

Conclusion
Bibliography
Index
Index of Case Studies

To my children, Alyssa and Christopher.

They are my inspiration.

ACKNOWLEDGEMENTS

A special thanks to my brother Brad. He has supported my professional pursuits with the highest degree of confidence.

And to my cousin, Philip Galdys, who provided the expertise and creativity necessary to ensure a professional text. To the family members who believed in me and continue to do so.

Early in my career I was fortunate to encounter very dedicated and skilled investigators. They guided me through a very difficult and complex justice system. I was taught to remain objective and impartial at all times. I learned to maintain a safe distance from the emotional hazards of investigative work. I understood that an investigator is a tool in the criminal justice system designed to seek out and uncover the truth. The investigator is not jury, judge, or executioner. The investigator is simply an objective and impartial practitioner of truth and justice. I now strive to offer the same level of wisdom to my many students. We all require guidance at one time or another. One can only hope that the guidance we receive is grounded in honor, integrity, and truth.

My sincere appreciation to Gene Bell and all of the many fine investigators, attorneys, and teachers who have influenced my career.

The assistance and contribution of Dr. Richard Grego requires special notice. The foreword written by Dr. Grego is an insightful prelude to the underlying theme of this text. However, his influence as a philosophical mentor is his greatest contribution.

I would also like to thank Mr. F. Lee Bailey. His recommendation and professional acknowledgement of my ability inspired me with a renewed confidence.

"It is better that ten
guilty persons escape,
than one innocent suffer."

- SIR WILLIAM BLACKSTONE

ABOUT THE AUTHOR

Brandon A. Perron is a licensed private investigator and the President of Investigative Support Specialist, Inc. Based in Fort Pierce Florida he has been qualified as an expert in the area of criminal investigation and specializes in criminal justice consulting, expert witness testimony, and training. He began his career in 1985 as a criminal investigator with the United States Air Force. He earned a degree in Criminal Justice and is a graduate of numerous military and civilian criminal investigation training programs. Upon departing the Air Force he was awarded several commendations and awards including the United States Air Force Commendation Medal for his "professional approach to crime solving." His career continued as a criminal investigator with the Florida 19th Judicial Circuit Public Defender's Office assigned to provide investigative support to the felony division. He departed the Public Defender's Office and established Investigative Support Specialist, Inc.

Mr. Perron has gained distinction as the region's premiere private investigator assisting the area's finest criminal defense and trial lawyers with major crimes and high profile media cases. He has investigated over 1000 criminal cases including over 100 homicide cases and 35 1st Degree Murder cases involving the death penalty. The painstaking efforts of Mr. Perron and his staff have cleared over 300 defendants falsely accused of a crime and countless cases resulting in reduced charges and attractive plea bargains. As publisher and editor he founded the ***CONFIDENTIAL INFORMANT CRIME MAGAZINE***, a publication focused on Florida crime and social issues. He has written numerous articles addressing the issues of crime, social problems, and criminal investigation appearing in industry publications such as ***P.I. MAGAZINE***. In 1994 he structured and organized the Florida 19th Judicial Circuit Public Defender investigations division and was appointed the Training Program Director. In 1995 Mr. Perron was appointed by Florida Governor Lawton Chiles to conduct investigations of suspected human and civil rights violations.

In 1998 ***P.I. MAGAZINE*** named Brandon Perron one of the top ten leading private investigators in the United States. He continues to train the investigative staff of the Public Defender as well as write and lecture on the subject of criminal investigation.

In 2000 Brandon Perron founded the ***Criminal Defense Investigation Training Council*** and the ***Board Certified Criminal Defense Investigator Program***. The council is responsible for the development of college level training programs focused upon the discipline of criminal defense investigation.

FOREWORD

It is perhaps surprising that this work on the science and methodology of criminal defense investigation is the first of its kind in current investigative literature. The Department of Justice reports that, during 1996, there were over 15 million arrests in the United States and over one million felony convictions alone. The prison population has been increasing at an average rate of eight percent per year over the past decade and is expected to increase by 43% over the next five years. Such statistics indicate the obvious need--in a judicial system that seeks to promote genuine legal equality--for defendants in criminal cases to receive responsible representation despite the bureaucratic limitations and human failings of due process. And just as essential to this representation as a good lawyer is a good investigator.

The renowned Defense Attorney F. Lee Bailey, who began his own career as an investigator, has often said that a good investigator is generally more valuable to a defendant's case than a good lawyer. Having worked as Lead Investigator with F. Lee Bailey, Brandon Perron shares this sentiment and can appreciate the professional context from which it derives. Mr. Perron's experience as a criminal investigator, in both the public and private sectors (for law enforcement as well as defense counsel), has cumulated in a course of study which he utilizes in his role as Trainer for the investigative staff of the Office of the Public Defender in the 19th Judicial Circuit of the State of Florida.

This book is an outline of and companion to the training program. It is also a reference and introductory guide to the field of criminal defense investigation. It is the only current work devoted exclusively to this specialty and thus provides the only comprehensive and methodical procedure for conducting criminal defense investigations that has yet been published. In this way it addresses an important and long-neglected need in the professional community.

Realizing this, Mr. Perron sets out to accomplish several things. One, of course, is to bring his extensive experience to bear upon the task of communicating a rigorous and pragmatic method for conducting any criminal defense investigation from beginning to end. This component method also known as "The Perron Method" was designed with both the skilled veteran and unskilled novice in mind. His book illustrates how even experienced law enforcement officers and investigators in other areas may have much to learn about a field for which there has, hitherto, been no formal training. The book also provides a point of departure from which new investigators can enter the field confidently. Both veterans and novices attend and benefit from his course.

Another goal of this book, course, and work generally, is to help elevate a profession that already enjoys a high standard of intellectual acuity, to an even higher level. Understanding that good criminal defense investigators must be critical thinkers in the truest sense, he envisions investigative work as being as much an exercise in challenging philosophical assumptions and opening the mind as it is a methodical routine. Indeed, Mr. Perron's grasp of philosophical epistemologies and perspectives on truth is exemplary. He is also well-read in history and the humanistic disciplines. What is really unusual though, is his ability to apply these skills and knowledge to practical investigative procedure. It is this ability that enables him to explore the process of criminal investigation on a level not often encountered in the field. It is unusual to engage a thinker who is equally comfortable interviewing an accused criminal on the street or delivering a lecture on theories of truth to a college philosophy class. It is rarer still to engage one who recognizes the profound and practical relationships between these kinds of activities.

Brandon Perron is such a thinker. It is his capacity to integrate deep philosophical reflection with investigative technique and critical thinking skills that has made him so successful in his profession. And it is this talent that he intends to share here--The monumental creative challenge of uncovering reasonable doubt demands no less.

Richard Grego M.A., D.A.
Department of Social/Behavioral Sciences
Indian River Community College

“

I hear much of people's
calling out to punish the guilty,
but very few are concerned
to clear the innocent.

-DANIEL DEFOE

Criminal defense investigation is and has been one of the most prestigious, challenging, and rewarding areas of investigation. The very nature and scope of the criminal defense investigation places it in a class of its own. The statement "my life is in your hands" is commonly uttered to the criminal defense investigator. This responsibility should not fall upon deaf ears. Nor should it fall upon unqualified ears. The criminal defense investigator must be experienced and capable of performing what most would call the impossible. Including, but not limited to, saving an innocent human being from the ultimate sentence: The death penalty.

The criminal defense investigator should only be concerned with seeking and pursuing the truth. Maintaining the very delicate balance on the scales of justice is a noble cause by any standard. Not unlike law enforcement officers, criminal defense investigators are confronted with the consequences of crime on a daily basis. However, the criminal defense investigator is provided with the opportunity to observe the effects of crime on our society from a different perspective.

In a perfect world every crime would be investigated thoroughly. Every lead would be pursued leaving no stone unturned. However, ours is not a perfect world. Therefore, criminal defense investigators are often shouldered with the awesome responsibility of bringing to light what others may not want to be uncovered. Many an innocent man has been condemned in the name of justice. Human beings by their very nature make mistakes, are often influenced and motivated by greed, and can be persuaded to pursue agendas other than that of the common good. Unfortunately, the pursuit of justice and a crime free society does not come without a high price. In fact, for some the price is often too high. An effective criminal defense investigator can ensure that fewer innocent people are forced to pay the price. In the words of Sir William Blackstone, "It is better that ten guilty persons escape, than one innocent suffer."

This manual was developed as a basic guide and reference source for the novice and experienced investigator interested in pursuing this honorable area of expertise. The criminal defense investigator should utilize this manual to navigate through the difficult and complex arena of criminal defense investigation. Interestingly enough, investigators who have compiled years of experience and enjoy credible reputations will often find themselves in a dilemma when confronted with a criminal defense assignment. Criminal defense investigations present many abstract issues and often do not reflect a clear beginning or end to the investigation process. With this in mind, the basic components of criminal defense investigation have been outlined in an easy to follow format. The basic components have been presented as a formula to conducting a successful and comprehensive criminal defense investigation. It is recommended that the outline be followed as a step by step guide. Each component of the investigation process is designed to provide leads and develop questions leading to the next component. The subsequent components will support the investigator's efforts to track leads and answer questions developed in the previous components. Utilizing this manual as a guide will allow the criminal defense investigator to begin and end a criminal defense investigation with the knowledge and confidence that a comprehensive and professional investigation was completed.

Of course, no guide can address every possible situation. Therefore, it is important for the criminal defense investigator to rely upon experience, training, good judgement, and common sense.

CHAPTER

1

THE CRIMINAL INVESTIGATOR'S PURVIEW

"

First, eliminate the impossible, whatever is left, however improbable, must be the truth.

- SIR ARTHUR CONAN DOYLE

Criminal investigations conducted by law enforcement agencies are designed to detect and apprehend criminals. In theory, law enforcement investigations are conducted in a systematic and impartial manner to uncover the truth. Law enforcement investigators conduct investigations to determine if a crime has been committed and to uncover evidence leading to who committed the crime. Based on the evidence uncovered, a suspect is identified and arrested. Subsequently, evidence uncovered by law enforcement investigators is presented to the prosecution. Again, based on the evidence uncovered a suspect is charged with the crime.

Criminal investigations are also conducted by the defense. Defense investigations must also be conducted in a systematic and impartial manner to uncover the truth. However, defense investigators generally do not need to determine if a crime was committed. Nor do they generally need to determine who has committed the crime. Defense investigations are often focused on specific issues, the goal being to uncover evidence to support that someone did not commit the crime. Specifically, that the defendant charged with the crime is not guilty. This goal can be met by uncovering reasonable doubt. To law enforcement and defense investigators alike the definition of reasonable doubt is often as confusing as the concept it represents. According to Black's Law Dictionary, reasonable doubt refers to "the degree of certainty required for a juror to legally find a criminal defendant not guilty". The official definition appears to provide little if any insight. Analysis of the term itself and defining the words "reasonable" and "doubt" individually may provide assistance. Reasonable, according to Webster's Dictionary, is defined as "Able to proceed, step by step, in thought, to a proper conclusion; governed by sound sense, moderate; acceptable". Webster's defines doubt as "lack of certainty about a fact or theory". Therefore, it is possible that reasonable doubt could be defined as "a conclusion of uncertainty regarding a specific fact or theory which was reached utilizing a sound, logical, and methodical thought process". Obviously, the concept of reasonable doubt is difficult to understand as well as define in simple terms. Attempts to identify or measure doubt to a degree of "reasonable" can be just as difficult. No proven method or scientific device is available to assist in this regard. Harvard law professor and legal scholar Alan Dershowitz provides an interesting method for determining reasonable doubt. He stated that if a juror believes a defendant is "probably" guilty - he must aquit. Believing that it is probable that one is guilty but not "reasonably" certain and being required to aquit is a very high standard. The highest standard in the world. Therefore, it would appear that one must properly and effectively consider all of the evidence and information available to be certain that a defendant is guilty - beyond a reasonable doubt.

In many cases, the criminal defense investigator will pursue reasonable doubt by scrutinizing specific aspects of the prosecution's case. Establishing that the prosecution's case is weak or deficient in a key area can be of great importance. The criminal defense investigator may also be called upon to conduct a comprehensive investigation, support a defendant's alibi, develop alternative suspects, or pursue other potential defense theories. Without question, the criminal defense investigator's role as a member of the defense is as difficult as it is crucial. Therefore, it is important for the criminal defense investigator to understand that his focus is to uncover reasonable doubt - not create it.

A systematic examination and inquiry of a criminal case is conducted by trained criminal defense investigators. In order to achieve a systematic and impartial investigation; defense investigators review the law enforcement investigation, interview the defendant, locate and interview witnesses, examine the crime scene, conduct background investigations, write reports, testify, and assist defense counsel with trial preparation. The result of an effective and successful investigation is not only limited to use in trial. Evidence uncovered by the criminal defense investigator may also result in a lower bond, reduced charges, or the dismissal of charges.

The basic criminal defense investigation can be accomplished by following specific investigative components defining the course of the investigation. The following text is designed as a guide and should be followed pursuant to the request of defense counsel.

The following guide is designed to provide criminal defense investigators with the fundamental knowledge and direction necessary to conduct a basic criminal defense investigation. Following the enclosed investigative outline and procedures, investigators will follow proven methods developed by experienced criminal defense investigators. Proper training is essential to the success of every investigator. Therefore, each investigator must be willing to dedicate the time and effort required to achieve the knowledge and skills necessary to succeed.

It is very important for a criminal defense investigator to maintain the highest degree of ethical conduct at all times. The following standards should be followed while performing in the official capacity of a criminal defense investigator:

1. Conduct all investigative tasks in a professional, ethical, and moral manner.
2. Conduct investigations within the limits of the law.
3. Remain impartial and objective at all times.
4. Protect and do not discuss confidential information with anyone other than designated individuals.

A successful criminal defense investigator should also possess and develop specific skills. These skills, if employed correctly, will enable the criminal defense investigator to achieve the highest standard of professionalism.

The criminal defense investigator should develop and hone the following skills in order to achieve the maximum degree of effectiveness

1. The ability to gain respect and cooperation.
2. The ability to uncover evidence and obtain complete statements from victims, witnesses, defendants, and suspects.
3. The ability to detect and uncover discrepancies and inconsistencies during the course of an interview.
4. The ability to record accurate, concise, and detailed notes.
5. The ability to connect intervals of time and actions.
6. The ability to develop contacts and sources of information.
7. The ability to accomplish accurate diagrams and photographs.
8. The ability to collect, process, identify, and classify evidence.
9. The ability and discretion to call upon experts in the evaluation of evidence.

10. The ability to accurately and clearly testify in court with credibility.

THE BASIC COMPONENTS OF CRIMINAL DEFENSE INVESTIGATION

The following components of investigative procedure should be used as a basic guide and formula when conducting a criminal defense investigation. The procedures can be amended or expanded to suit the individual needs of each case. The proceedure is designed to apply effectively to all criminal defense cases from simple battery to first degree murder.

1. Investigative Review of the discovery file; police reports, victim/witness statements, crime scene examinations, lab reports, etc.
2. Initial Defendant Interview.
3. Crime Scene Examination, Diagram, & Photography.
4. Victim/Witness Background Investigation.
5. Witness Location, Interviews, and Statements.
6. Report of Investigation & Testifying

The criminal defense investigator will not always be required to pursue all of the procedures outlined within this text. However, he should fully understand each and be able to effectively accomplish each task if called upon to do so.

CHAPTER

2

The Search for Truth: Critical Thinking for the Criminal Defense Investigator

"

There is no better way of
exercising the imagination
than the study of law.
No poet ever interpreted
nature as freely as a lawyer
interprets the truth.

-JEAN GIRARDOUX

Truth as a concept or idea has been debated and studied for thousands of years. The great philosophers pursuit of truth has been well documented and studied for centuries. The question: "Do you swear to tell the truth, the whole truth, and nothing but the truth?" is daily echoed within the halls of our criminal justice system. However, one wonders how many people can successfully distinguish truth from error. A poll of 100 potential jurors would probably find 100 people confident that they could determine the truth. But the question is "Whose truth would they find?"

The methodology for determining truth is not simple and unproblematic. The average person encounters questions of truth and error on a daily basis. However, the methods used to address these questions are as diverse as the cultures and unique experiences of each individual. Therefore, the methods used by each individual investigator can be as diverse as the human population. It is true that the technical guidelines and procedures accepted by the investigative industry are generally similar in design. The problem lies not in the technical recovery of facts, but in the philosophical definition of truth. Before one can embark on a successful journey to uncover the truth, an effective plan of action and method must be conceived. Such a methodology might be described as a philosophy.

Investigation and philosophy have a great deal in common. Philosophy, technically defined, is the critical evaluation of all the facts of experience. This definition would apply to the investigator, who must critically evaluate all investigative facts in order to uncover the truth. In this definition, "critical evaluation" implies that the philosopher must consider all information with rigorous scrutiny, dismissing bias and prejudice of any kind. Thus, it is not unreasonable to claim that, in many ways, the investigator is something of a practical philosopher.

The scientific community contends that they alone are the keepers of the search for truth within the criminal justice system. Unfortunately, the scientists' pursuit of truth is as limited as their imagination. They present recent developments and breakthroughs in forensic science as examples and evidence of their truth. Yet one need only be an amateur student of history to know that truth, as defined by the scientific community, changes with the results of every new experiment and with the development of every new, and yet to be proven, theory. For example, as recently as the nineteenth century, leading criminologists accepted as true that criminals were born as such and could be identified by facial characteristics specific to their law-breaking tendencies. Such a theory sounds utterly ridiculous to the twentieth century criminal justice professional. One can only wonder what criminal justice practitioners of the twenty-first century will think of DNA fingerprinting. Only time will tell. The one thing we know for sure is that, whatever the future holds, our descendants will probably also believe that they have discovered the truth.

The primary term which most accurately describes the investigator/philosopher's role is evaluation. The investigator/philosopher evaluates every fact of experience available. The scientist focuses upon selected facts which lie within his specific field of study.

Like a scientist, the investigator must determine and identify a criterion of truth. A criterion, test, standard, or rule to judge the accuracy of information must be effectively followed as a verification process. All human beings have and continue to implement many methods and tests to determine truth. The investigator should be aware of many methods available in order to understand perspectives of others when they present him with information which they believe to be true.

The following represents many of the methods utilized to determine the truth:

1. Custom/Tradition - Many intentionally or without thought employ this method. The belief that a fact is "customary" or a "tradition," and therefore is the truth, can be very comforting.

2. Time - "It has stood the test of time, so it must therefore be true"

is commonly heard in many cultures.

3. Feelings - Many people base the truth on what they "feel." Such a determination is often made without any logical evaluation of the facts.

4. Instinct - Instinctive behavior within human beings has been studied for ages. The basic instinct to seek shelter or food when one is hungry does not necessarily qualify it as an accurate verification method.

5. Hunch/Intuition - Such impulses are generally vague and without a basis in reasoning or consideration of facts.

6. Majority Rule - A statistical basis for the acceptance of truth. Utilized by democratic societies as a criterion for truth.

7. Naive Realism - Based upon the belief that human senses determine the truth of an object or idea. In other words, only that which is subject to first hand observation is verifiable.

8. Correspondence - This holds that an idea which agrees with its object is true. For example, the idea that the Liberty Bell is in Philadelphia is true because its location in Philadelphia corresponds with the idea.

9. Authority - The opinions of highly educated professionals within their specific disciplines are often regarded as acceptable sources of the truth. The use of experts within the criminal justice system is commonly utilized as a criterion of truth.

10. Pragmatic - "If it works, it must be true."

11. Coherence - The coherence theory states that all the facts must be in proper relationship to one another consistently and cohesively as parts of an integrated whole. Whatever facts are uncovered must be explained and effectively integrated in the system as a relevant facet of that system. Consider a jigsaw puzzle. Not only must all the pieces be uncovered, but they must properly conform to one another and present a clear discernible picture upon completion.

12. Existentialism - Existentialism holds that there is no single rational method or formula for ascertaining the truth because methods and formulas are imperfect constructs of the finite human intellect while truth itself is infinite and unknowable. Truth can be realized directly in the immediacy of living experience but it can only be represented indirectly by intellectual ideas about experience. Therefore, truth depends less upon exactly what you believe and more upon the spirit in which you live-out your beliefs.

In order to effectively pursue the truth, the investigator must be able to define it. Such a task would appear to be quite simple. However, it is much more difficult than generally believed. The first question an investigator should ask himself is whether or not he believes that truth is relative or absolute. The debate over this question has raged since the days of Socrates.

The sophist Protagoras of Abdera is probably the most historically recognized supporter of the theory that truth is relative. He based his determination on the fact that man's knowledge and experience are flawed due to the imperfection of human senses. (Consider that even the utilization of sense enhancing equipment is an inadequate method of discerning truth because of limited advancements in technology.) Therefore, relative truth is merely a subjective opinion. What is true for you is only true for you.

The theory of truth as absolute can be just as puzzling. Many claim that there is only one absolute truth. However, a close examination of this perspective usually reveals relativism in disguise. An absolutist claims that his truth is absolute. However, this is merely his opinion and, as such, it can never be verified absolutely. So, in actuality, his truth is relative. It should also be noted that the relativist finds himself in the same quandary. He is expressing an absolute truth when he claims that truth is relative and not absolute. He thus contradicts himself by essentially admitting that truth is absolute and not relative.

In light of this paradox, perhaps the investigator should pursue the truth as a concept which is absolute--realizing that because of his inherent flaws and imperfections, he may never find it. Aspiring to such a level of perfection can only benefit the investigator and the criminal justice system. Truth may very well be to the investigator what the Holy Grail was to the crusader. Simply an ideal.

Obviously than, the criminal defense investigator must--from either an absolutist or a relativist standpoint--elevate his critical thinking ability to a level of intellectual awareness attained by very few. Accept this endeavor as a challenge which must be met effectively and a goal which must be achieved. Professionally speaking, it is a matter of life and death.

CHAPTER

3

Investigative Case Review & Analysis
Investigative Outline
Investigative Journal

COMPONENT ONE

"

In the field of observation,
chance favors only the
prepared minds.

-LOUIS PASTEUR

The Investigative Case Review is arguably the most important element of the criminal defense investigation. In defense investigation, every action requires a reaction. The criminal defense investigator must be completely aware of exactly what the allegations in question entail. In order to effectively contest the evidence presented by the prosecution, one must be knowledgeable of all the facts and evidence involved in the case. Only then, will the criminal defense investigator be able to scrutinize the prosecution's evidence and react accordingly. Renowned criminal defense attorney and former investigator, F. Lee Bailey, states "Hard evidence, rather than abstract legal argument is what decides most criminal cases. You must be fully in command of the facts in order to be fully in command of a case. Do not let the prosecution surprise you by any of its evidence." With this in mind, prior to conducting any investigative tasks, including interviewing the defendant, a thorough investigative review of the discovery file should be accomplished. At a minimum, the arrest affidavit, offense reports, and supplemental reports should be reviewed in order to gain knowledge of the specific allegations, evidence, and witnesses.

The criminal defense investigator must pursue evidence to disprove the elements of the alleged crime or at a minimum uncover evidence to support reasonable doubt. With this in mind, the criminal defense investigator should review the legal aspects of the alleged crime and identify the specific elements which the prosecution must prove to obtain a conviction. Remember, the defense is not burdened to prove that the defendant did not commit the alleged crime or act. The defense must reveal that the prosecution's case is deficient in that it does not, beyond a reasonable doubt, establish the proper premise or foundation necessary to obtain a conviction.

A thorough review of the police reports will enable the criminal defense investigator to conduct a thorough interview of the defendant, victim, and witnesses, and will also provide the knowledge and perspective necessary to accomplish an effective examination of the crime scene. Thorough knowledge of the allegations, evidence, and statements provided by witnesses can provide substantial assistance in identifying contradictory statements or evidence disputing the prosecution's evidence.

Review of the police reports requires more than just reading the reports. The average person does not retain what he reads and will merely view the documents, retaining little, if any specifics. Therefore, the criminal defense investigator should carefully review the police reports in a methodical manner. The criminal defense investigator should scrutinize each document line by line and page by page. In addition, it can be very beneficial to take notes or highlight specific information with a marker for reference purposes. An effective investigation begins with a properly conducted investigative case review to uncover discrepancies, leads, and additional questions which can only be answered through further investigation.

Keep in mind, the investigative case review should not only attempt to detect the obscure. Historically, the investigator tends to overlook the obvious, often overlooking valuable evidence. The very definition of the term "detect", according to Webster's Dictionary is "to discover, to bring to light, especially something obscure." Therefore, by their very nature the investigator often overlooks the obvious in search of the obscure. With this in mind, it is very important for the criminal defense investigator to look at the entire picture. Criminal cases should be viewed as a puzzle and carefully examined. Like a puzzle, every piece of the investigation, no matter how large or small, should be compared to the "big picture." However, before attempting to put the puzzle together one must be sure to have all of the pieces. Failure to obtain all of the necessary pieces may distort the final product failing to assemble a true representation of the "big picture."

Utilizing the following exercise the criminal defense investigator can identify his ability to detect the obscure without overlooking the obvious.

INVESTIGATION SCENARIO/PRACTICAL EXERCISE

Crime: Murder
Location: Mountainside State Park
Victim: Mary Harris
Suspect: Jim Smith
Witness: Albert Ryan

The following is an excerpt from the initial police report reflecting the statement of the eye witness identified as Albert Ryan.

"On Monday, January 15, 1995, at 6:55 pm, 911 received an emergency call for assistance to the Mountainside State Park. At 7:25 pm, The suspect, Jim Smith, was discovered by rescue personnel in a ravine approximately 100 feet below the edge of a steep cliff. The Medical Examiner arrived on the scene at 7:43 pm, and determined the cause of death to have been the result of a fall. He noted the reddish-purple discoloration of post mortem lividity Mortis was in its early stages, estimating the Suspect, Jim Smith, had been dead approximately 2 hours. The suspect was found clothed in a one piece blue in color ski suit, ankle high leather hiking boots, socks, mitts, scarf, a woolen cap, two shirts, and long thermal underwear. The victim was found by police in a campsite approximately 100' above and to the north of the suspect's body. At 8:20 pm the medical examiner arrived at the campsite and noted contusions to the victim's head and neck. He determined the cause of death to have been caused by a blunt instrument. Based on observations of post mortem lividity the medical examiner estimated the victim had been killed five to six hours earlier. At 7:40 pm, Detectives interviewed the eye witness, identified as Albert Ryan, who provided the following statement; "I returned to the campsite before dark at approximately 5:45 pm to help Mary Harris start a fire and assist with dinner, after departing the campsite at 7:30 am and hiking most of the day. Upon arriving at the camp, I observed Jim Smith and Mary Harris engaged in a heated argument. They had been together for several years and often held heated discussions. I maintained a safe distance to avoid detection in an attempt to mind my own business and spare the couple embarrassment. After approximately ten minutes the argument intensified. Without warning Jim Smith retrieved a large ax and struck Mary with a fatal blow to the head. Alarmed, I shouted, alerting Jim Smith to my presence. Startled, he turned and ran in the opposite direction. Unfortunately, it would appear he had forgotten about the cliff and tragically fell to his death. I then immediately hiked down the mountain trail and telephoned 911 for help." The ax was forwarded to the crime lab for examination. Forensic examination uncovered the fingerprints of Jim Smith on the ax handle.

Careful examination and scrutinization of the police report would uncover a number of leads and questions to be answered by further investigation. However, one specific item of interest is able to remain obscure as well as obvious. Review of the report utilizing a line by line method without losing site of the entire picture should detect a major investigative question. The suspect, Jim Smith, was discovered wearing mitts. The lab identified the finger prints of Jim Smith on the ax that killed Mary Harris. How did the finger prints of Jim Smith get on the ax if he was wearing mitts? A serious question which could have been overlooked without a proper investigative review of the case.

THE INVESTIGATIVE TIME LINE

Another investigative tool often used by experienced criminal defense investigators is a time line of major events relevant to the allegations in question. A properly prepared time line can assist the criminal defense investigator with the organization of information and facts. For example, as a criminal defense investigation evolves additional information and witnesses will be added to the equation. The times and dates of relevant activity and witness observations will be added to an already complex investigation. Proper organization, referencing, and cross-referencing, will become necessary in order to classify information and evidence. A time line of major events will provide a reference tool clearly defining the relationship of specific activity and events with other evidence and witness testimony. A properly prepared and developed time line can also be used as an investigative tool by the criminal defense investigator and defense counsel. It should be noted that time lines will change as new evidence is uncovered and additional witnesses are interviewed. Therefore, the time line should be up-dated on a regular basis to reflect new information. The criminal defense investigator should also be prepared to recognize a flaw in the defense theory or investigative strategy. A time line will reveal specific evidence and testimony inconsistent with facts. Such inconsistencies may favor the defense or the prosecution. Effectively prepared, the time line may also be used as a defense exhibit. It may be introduced at trial to assist defense counsel with direct and cross examination of witnesses or in opening and closing arguments.

The following example time line is intended as a guide and is based on the facts of the Practical Exercise.

TIME LINE OF EVENTS AND FACTS

```
7:30 am -  Eye Witness/Albert Ryan departs campsite.

2:20 pm to
3:20 pm -  Medical Examiner's estimated time of death for the
           Victim/Mary Harris.

5:21 pm -  Sunset.  (Source:  Mountainside Gazette)

5:43 pm -  Medical Examiner's estimated time of death for the
           Suspect/Jim Smith.

5:45 pm -  Eye Witness/Albert Ryan returns to campsite.

5:55 pm -  Suspect/Jim Smith Strikes fatal blow to
           Victim/Mary Harris's head. (Time based on estimate
           of 10 minutes provided by Eye Witness/Albert Ryan)
```

6:35 pm - 911 receives emergency call.

7:00 pm - Suspect/Jim Smith's body is found at bottom of ravine.

7:43 pm - Medical examiner arrives on scene and examines the body of Suspect/Jim Smith.

7:40 pm - Detectives interview the Eye Witness/Albert Ryan.

8:20 pm - Medical examiner examines body of the Victim/Mary Harris.

Information and details reflected within police reports are often confusing and difficult to understand dependent upon the writing style of the officer responsible for the report. Therefore, classification of the data by accomplishing a time line of major relevant events noted within reports can be very beneficial to the criminal defense investigator. Again, a time line of major events will provide a reference tool clearly defining the relationship of specific activity and events with other evidence and witness testimony.

The example time line developed from Scenario A is a fine example of how a properly prepared time line can provide the investigator with valuable insight. For example review of the time line revealed two very obvious inconsistencies;

1. Witness Albert Ryan related that he returned to the campsite during daylight, around 5:45 pm. However, as reflected in the time line, sunset was at 5:21 pm. Indicating that he may have returned earlier than he reported.

2. Witness Albert Ryan estimated Mary Harris' time of death at approximately 5:55 pm. However, the medical examiner estimated her time of death between 2:20 pm and 3:20 pm.

As reflected in Scenario A, the time line is based on information reflected within the police reports and statements provided by witnesses. As additional information is uncovered the time line will change. As the time line changes a clear picture of the facts will develop. A clear picture of the facts and evidence will provide the criminal defense investigator with a sense of direction for the investigation.

When confronted with a substantial or voluminous amount of documents criminal defense investigators must be cautious not to merely scan for significant information. A cursory scan often results in the criminal defense investigator missing crucial facts. Therefore, documentary evidence must be studied carefully with a very discriminating eye. The study method is best accomplished with a plan or philosophy. The information being examined should be organized for maximum effectiveness and comprehension.

Information can be classified and organized into five basic categories;

1. Time - Chronological order of events.

2. Alphabetically.

3. Location.

4. Topic.

5. Continuum or magnitude scale.

Each of the five methods provides a different perspective of the information and data being examined. Therefore, approaching the information from a different angle may uncover inconsistencies, leads, or additional questions. Utilizing one or more of the methods described will provide an effective cross-reference tool to check the information with painstaking attention to detail and scrutiny. Proper and effective investigative review and analysis of a case file can turn the mere reading of documents into a thought provoking process.

The criminal defense investigator should also be prepared to conduct extensive research and study when confronted with evidence, information, terminology, or situations foreign to him. Additional research regarding forensic science disciplines may be necessary in order to familiarize oneself with proper procedure. The criminal defense investigator may also be required to call upon various experts in the evaluation of evidence presented by the prosecution and encountered in the field.

It is important to note that the investigative case review and analysis is not limited to documentary evidence. Review of the evidence list identifying and describing the physical evidence should be followed by an examination of the actual physical evidence. Close inspection of the physical evidence is required to determine if it in fact corresponds with the description presented by the prosecution. A physical inspection of the evidence will also confirm the existence and proper maintenance of such evidence. It is not uncommon to find that physical evidence has been destroyed, lost, or misplaced. Inspection may also discover the existence of additional exculpatory evidence which was not reflected within the evidence list. Careful review, analysis, and inspection of all the prosecution's evidence is a crucial component of an effective criminal defense investigation.

The following is an example of how an effective investigative case review of the prosecution's evidence can assist defense counsel:

CASE STUDY: HOMICIDE/1ST DEGREE MURDER

The prosecution's case against the defendant accused in the stabbing death of an Alabama man unraveled when a private investigator retained by the defense uncovered that prosecution witnesses provided nine documented versions of the incident. The defendant could have faced the death penalty if a Florida jury had convicted him of murder. The defendant was arrested in 1991 for the stabbing death of a 25 year old male. The victim was beaten and knifed during a drunken brawl which began as a friendly barbecue. The case appeared to be air tight until the defense investigator began to scrutinize the volumes of testimonial evidence provided by the prosecution. Specifically, the private investigator revealed that three witnesses changed their stories dramatically each time they were interviewed. The investigative case review reflected that the testimony of the witnesses was plagued with inaccuracy and inconsistency. For example, one of the witnesses said that during the attack she was sitting outside by the barbecue which is right in front of where the stabbing occurred. She added that the attack occurred inside the residence. However, there was never any question that the stabbing took place outside based on the presence of blood evidence and additional witness testimony. The witness also changed the location of the stabbing three times in three separate interviews with police. The defense investigator uncovered that two of the witnesses, who claimed to be eye witnesses, were confirmed alcoholics and suffered from blackouts and consumed about a case of beer prior to the altercation. A plea bargain was reached based on several mitigating factors including evidence uncovered by the defense investigator. The defendant avoided the death penalty and was sentenced to 40 years in prison.

THE INVESTIGATIVE OUTLINE

Upon completing the investigative case review and developing a time line it is advisable to accomplish an investigative outline. The investigative outline can organize and categorize questions and leads uncovered during the investigative case review. The outline can also provide the criminal defense investigator with a sense of direction and clearly defined plan of action. This will maximize the criminal defense investigator's chances of success and minimize the possibility of forsaking the pursuit of important leads or questions.

The following example outline is intended as a guide for the proper preparation of criminal defense investigation cases.

1. Case Preparation and Review.
   A. Conference with defense counsel.
      a. Identify preliminary theory of defense.
   B. Conduct Investigative Case Review.
   C. Prepare a time line of major events.
   D. Prepare investigative outline defining the direction of the investigation and submit to defense counsel.

2. Initial Defendant Interview.
   A. Conduct a complete initial defendant interview.
   B. Identify potential defense witnesses.
   C. Written report and submit to defense counsel.

3. Examine the Crime Scene.
   A. Photograph & diagram scene.
   B. Write report and submit to defense counsel.

4. Identify and Classify Prosecution & Defense Witnesses.
   A. Assemble file for each witness.
   B. Accomplish background investigations.

5. Locate and Interview Witnesses.

6. Compare Witness Statements to Previous Statements.
   A. Write report and submit to defense counsel.

7. Conduct Follow-up Investigation Based on Investigative Results and Request of Defense Counsel.
   A. Write final report and submit to defense counsel.

As reflected within the example outline it would be wise to submit a copy of the investigative outline to defense counsel. Submission of the investigative outline will ensure defense counsel is aware of your strategy and activities. Remember, the criminal defense investigator must be fully knowledgeable of all the facts in order to prepare and conduct an effective investigation.

A reliable method of documenting the activity of a criminal defense investigator is to maintain an Investigation Journal. It is very important to maintain a record of the dates and times reflecting investigative efforts associated with each case. Documenting activity such as attempts to contact a witness, witness interviews, background investigations, crime scene examinations, and other investigative efforts can be very beneficial for future reference. Proper documentation will also attest to the credibility of the criminal defense investigator and the evidence uncovered as a result of investigation.

Criminal cases are frequently subjected to time delays often encountered in the criminal justice system. Because of overloaded docket schedules and continuances granted to the prosecution and defense, a criminal case can take months or sometimes years to go to trial. With this in mind, proper documentation of the criminal defense investigator's activity and efforts may not only be advisable but necessary in order to effectively testify.

A clear and accurate investigative journal will allow the criminal defense investigator to access times, dates, and activity with ease. Such displays of preparation and organization will only support the criminal defense investigator's credibility and ability in the eyes of the client, defense attorney, prosecutor, judge, and most importantly the jury.

The following is a sample Investigation Journal provided for reference:

SAMPLE INVESTIGATION JOURNAL

Reference:	**State of Florida Vs. John Doe**
Case No:	**95-0001-CF**
Type:	Burglary of a Dwelling
Attorney:	Joseph Johnson, Attorney At Law
Investigator:	Thomas Jones, Investigator

02/18/95	-	Reviewed case file.
	-	Interviewed defendant at county jail.
02/21/95	-	Examine crime scene, diagram scene, and photograph. Drop off photographs to be developed.
02/22/95	-	Conduct background investigations of potential witnesses at county courthouse.
02/25/95	-	Attempt to contact witness Al Brown at home, 123 Avenue H, Ft. Pierce, at 2 pm, attempted again at 4:30 pm. Spoke with neighbor who related witness works days and is usually home after 7 pm.
02/25/95	-	Contacted and interviewed Al Brown at his residence at 7:30 pm. Obtained narrative statement from witness who was unwilling to provide a recorded statement.
02/26/95	-	Briefed defense counsel Joseph Johnson regarding investigative results, accomplished written report and submitted to defense counsel for review.

CHAPTER

4

Initial Defendant Interview

COMPONENT TWO

> The louder he talked of his honor, the faster we counted our spoons.
>
> **- RALPH WALDO EMERSON**

> It's the easiest thing in the world for a man to deceive himself.
>
> **- BENJAMIN FRANKLIN**

The initial defendant interview is a key element in the criminal defense investigation process. In effect, the interview of the defendant can make or break a case. Therefore, it is very important that the interview be conducted in a professional manner. As a criminal defense investigator and representative of defense counsel, the investigator must present himself as a professional. The dress, appearance, demeanor, and attitude of the criminal defense investigator must be beyond reproach.

Upon meeting with a defendant, the criminal defense investigator should immediately identify himself and provide the name of the attorney representing the defendant. The defendant should then be informed that the criminal defense investigator will be conducting the initial defendant interview and reporting the facts of the case to defense counsel. Establish a rapport with the defendant and confirm the element of confidentiality between the defendant, defense counsel, and the investigator. As a general rule, the communication between defense counsel and his agents retained to assist in the defense of a criminal case is protected under the attorney-client privilege and work product doctrine. The extension of the privilege to agents of defense counsel is commonly identified as the Kovel Privilege, deriving its name from the decision in the United States V. Kovel, 296 F.2d 918 (2d Cir. 1961). The privilege is subject to all of the customary limitations of the attorney-client privilege.

With this in mind, inform the defendant that it is in his best interest to be cooperative and completely honest in order to accomplish a successful investigation. Also, it should be strongly recommended that it is in the defendant's best interest that he not discuss the facts of his case with anyone else, as anything he might say could be discovered and subsequently used against him.

The criminal defense investigator should obtain the defendant's personal history information. The following guidelines can be followed in order to ensure all the necessary information required is obtained. It is not advisable to record the defendant's statement.

A. Obtain the defendant's personal information.
   1. Full name, date of birth, place of birth, social security number, and personal description such as height, weight, hair color, and eye color, etc.
   2. Present home address, prior addresses and dates of residency. Telephone number.
   3. Family members, spouse, children, etc., list full names and addresses.
   4. Employment information - present and past.
   5. Educational history and military service.
   6. criminal history & arrest record - disposition.
   7. Financial situation (bond hearing information).
   8. Medical history, psychiatric history, alcohol and drug use history.

B. Question the defendant thoroughly.
   1. If available allow the defendant to review the police report.
   2. Ask the defendant if he agrees or disagrees with the facts reflected within the police report.
   3. Allow the defendant to present his version of the facts: When, Where, What, Who, How, and Why?
   4. Obtain details of the events surrounding the allegations. Ask the defendant to describe the details and circumstances, including time and place, surrounding his arrest.
   5. Was the defendant under the influence of drugs or alcohol when arrested?
   6. Does the defendant know the victim? If yes, How?
   7. Has the defendant ever had any problems with the victim previously? If yes, describe in detail.
   8. Did the defendant provide a written or recorded statement to police? If yes, describe in detail. Did the defendant take a polygraph examination?
   9. Was the defendant asked to participate in a line-up?
   10. Did the police present the defendant with any evidence or statements to be used against him?

11. Did the police take any property from the defendant's person, residence, automobile, or place of employment? If yes, describe in detail.
12. Remember to use the questions, When, Where, What, Who, How, and Why?, as a guide.
13. Be a good listener.

In addition, other documents such as bond reduction forms, records release forms, and any additional documentation requested by defense counsel should be completed at this time. It is recommended that forms reflecting the questions covered be developed as a guide to assist the criminal defense investigator in the initial defendant interview process.

Prepared forms should be filled out in their entirety. Do not leave questions blank. In the event that a question does not apply to the defendant, write N/A (Not Applicable). Answers should be detailed and specific. All release forms should be completed and signed by the defendant in the presence of a notary public in the event they are needed by defense counsel.

THE POLYGRAPH: AN INVESTIGATIVE TOOL FOR THE CRIMINAL DEFENSE INVESTIGATOR

Historically, the polygraph has been utilized by law enforcement as an investigative tool to evaluate the truthfulness of suspects. Unquestionably, the most valuable aspect of polygraph testing has been to help exonerate the innocent defendant who has been a target of circumstantial evidence. The polygraph as an investigative tool is most valuable in cases relying heavily upon testimonial evidence to support the prosecution's position. With that in mind, the polygraph should not be overlooked by the defense. It is true that unless both the prosecution and the defense agree, the results of a polygraph examination are not admissible in court. However, successful polygraph results consistent with a criminal defendant's innocence can be very valuable to the defense. Strategically, the defense may utilize favorable results to convince a prosecutor to dismiss charges. Favorable results may also be utilized to reduce bail or negotiate a plea bargain.

Properly administered, the polygraph examination of a criminal defendant by the defense should be strictly confidential and administered under the protection of the attorney-client privilege. The very fact that a polygraph examination is being administered to the defendant should not be released. In the event that deception by the defendant is noted, the results of the examination can remain confidential and not be released to the prosecution.

Although often misunderstood, the theory of the polygraph is actually quite simple. The emotion of fear is the dominant factor in the psychology of lie detection. The fear of entrapment or exposure that is triggered by lying causes the individual to exhibit an autonomic uncontrollable reaction in relation to lying. The person trying to lie will display psychological reactions, which are uncontrollable, automatic, and can be recorded by the polygraph.

The question of accuracy regarding the polygraph has been debated for over 75 years in over 250 studies. However, according to the American Polygraph Association, "the preponderance of available information indicates that when a properly trained examiner utilizes an established testing procedure, the accuracy of the decisions made by the polygraph examiners is generally in the range of 85-95% for specific issue examinations." The opinion of the American Polygraph Association appears to support that the polygraph is only as good as it's examiner. Therefore, if a polygraph examination is to be administered to the defendant, it is very important to retain the services of a properly trained and experienced polygraph examiner.

Another instrument gaining distinction as an investigative tool to evaluate truthfulness is the voice stress analyzer or VSA. The specific objective of the VSA is to utilize the human voice to measure physiological response to psychological change . Depending upon the accepted practices within a specific jurisdiction, the VSA may also be utilized as a strategic tool in the same manner as a polygraph.

Of course, the polygraph and voice stress analyzer are testing the defendant's subjective opinion of what is true or false. The criterion of truth utilized by the defendant is not subject to the test nor is it measurable by scientific intruments.

The following case is just one example of how effective use of the polygraph, coupled with a thorough investigation, can give the defense an unbeatable combination.

CASE STUDY: SEXUAL BATTERY

The facts of the case were very interesting in that they were very similar to the facts in the nationally recognized rape trial of William Kennedy Smith, resulting in an acquittal in West Palm Beach, Florida. The defendant in this case, an affluent married young white male, had been arrested and charged with Sexual Battery. The complainant, a young white female, was alleging that he forced her to have sexual intercourse against her will. The incident allegedly occurred in the early morning hours on the beach behind a motel located on the east coast of Florida known as the Treasure Coast. The defendant admitted having sex with the woman, but claimed she was not only willing, but aggressively initiated the sexual activity. The defendant denied forcing her in any way to have sex with him.

He had met her earlier, at a local dance club, where he and a friend were out for a night on the town. She had been drinking, as had he, and after playing the ageless game of "cat and mouse," he and his friend agreed to give her a ride home. The trio departed the dance club together without incident. However, before bringing her home, they ended up in the motel parking lot where his friend had left his car earlier. Coincidentally, a police officer showed up at the scene, and after informally speaking with the defendant, told him to call for a ride, as he did not appear that he was sober enough to drive himself. Based on the police officer's recommendation, he entered the motel lobby to find a telephone. The woman followed him in and asked him to accompany her out the back door and onto the beach. He complied. Once on the beach, one thing led to another, resulting in the two having sex. He claimed that she initiated the sexual activity, administering oral sex upon him. Furthermore, he claimed that he was an unwilling participant due to the fact that not only had he been drinking, he was married, and felt guilty about the entire incident, thus limiting his ability to become fully aroused. However, he did arouse sufficiently to have sexual intercourse with her.

After having sexual intercourse, they returned separately to the parking lot. In addition, they encountered the police officer as they were leaving the beach. The woman, with ample opportunity, said nothing to the police officer. The defendant returned to the parking lot alone, rejoined his friend, and a few minutes later the officer and the female joined them. Again, the woman said nothing to the police officer, revealing no indication that a crime had just been committed. As a matter of fact, the officer ended up driving her home, after the defendant declined to do so. The defendant's refusal to provide the woman with a ride obviously angered her. The following day, the police arrived at the defendant's home and arrested him for Sexual Battery based on a complaint filed by the woman. Subsequently, the defendant hired an experienced trial lawyer known for his aggressive approach to criminal defense cases to defend his innocence.

The attorney retained the services of a private investigator to investigate the allegations on behalf of his client. The defense investigation was initiated prior to formal charges by the State Attorney's office. This provided the defense with an opportunity to present the State with evidence to support the defendant's innocence and with a little luck avoid further pursuit of the charges. After careful review of the allegations, an investigation team, consisting of three investigators, was assigned to investigate the allegations in question. The investigation consisted of a strategically planned systematic approach to witness location and interviews, examination of the physical evidence, background investigation, and surveillance of the alleged victim. Over 100 hours of painstaking investigation uncovered substantial evidence to support the defendant's innocence. A major break in the case occurred when the investigation team uncovered a witness and supporting documentation revealing that the alleged victim had made false allegations of sexual assault in the past. In addition, several witnesses were identified who were able to provide testimony supporting that the alleged victim's reputation for truthfulness in the community was less than credible. In fact, the alleged victim had a reputation for fabricating rumors and allegations regarding her "romantic interests." Furthermore, the alleged victim's attempts to project a "Shirley Temple" image was shattered by the investigation team's discovery that she was employed as as an exotic dancer a/k/a "stripper" in a local dancing establishment. Upon completing the field investigation, all the evidence was assembled and documented in a lengthy written report and submitted to defense counsel. Defense counsel presented the investigative results to the State prosecutor. After reviewing the evidence, the prosecutor related that if the defendant could pass a polygraph test by their examiner, he would probably drop the case.

Needless to say, the defense was a polygraph away from a major victory. However, defense counsel was not about to have the defendant tested without knowing the outcome beforehand. After all, for unknown reasons, clients are known to lie to their lawyers on a regular basis. With this in mind, a highly qualified and respected polygraph examiner was contracted to perform the confidential test before submitting the defendant to the law enforcement examination. The examiner, a recognized and certified polygraph expert, had been adjudged as an expert witness by various state and federal courts. Based on the examiner's prior results, the investigation team was confident that if the defendant could pass the stringent test administered by the polygraph examiner, he could pass any test, and so prove his innocence.

A series of tests were administered to the defendant, resulting in the examiner's determination that the defendant appeared to be telling the truth in denying he forced the woman to have sex with him. However, he felt that the defendant was holding back information that made the results less than ideal. Based upon these observations, the examiner concluded that the defendant should not submit to a law enforcement test until this issue was clarified. With the entire outcome of the case at stake, it was time to stop holding the defendant's hand and read him the "riot act." As stated earlier, defendants tend to be less than truthful with their defense attorneys. Therefore, defense investigators are often called upon to conduct "heart to heart" interviews with defendants on behalf of defense counsel. This was one of those times. The defendant was obviously not telling the whole truth. Although it was believed that he was innocent of the charges, it was also believed that he was holding back. Interestingly enough, obtaining confessions from a defendant can be as difficult for the defense as it is for law enforcement. However, the "heart to heart" paid off. The defendant indicated that he was not completely candid, and was not a less than willing participant in the sexual encounter. He related that he lied about his participation because he was concerned that his wife would become even further angered if she were to discover that he was a willing participant. This revelation was discussed with the polygraph examiner, who agreed that an outside issue such as this would effect the defendant's test results. Therefore, it was decided that the man would be re-tested after reviewing the circumstances again with him.

During the pre-test interview, it became apparent that the defendant was indeed a willing participant. However, after the sexual encounter was completed, he became uneasy and feeling guilty, he wanted to get way from her as quickly as possible. To add to the guilt, he was concerned about not being able to perform satisfactorily. In retrospect, the defendant believed that the woman was probably angry and humiliated, and this prompted her to make the complaint in order to get even with him. What probably made it worse was his refusal to give her a ride home after the encounter, resulting in the police officer having to do so, further humiliating her. The defendant was re-tested, this time passing with no reservations. The results were made known to the prosecutor, who then rightfully dropped pursuit of Sexual Battery charges without subjecting the defendant to a polygraph test by law enforcement. Based on the thoroughness of the investigation team and the polygraph examiner, the matter was brought to a swift and successful conclusion and justice was served. Had the client been allowed to take the law enforcement test without clearing up the areas of concern, he may easily have been found deceptive, resulting in further pursuit of the charges and a possible trial.

CHAPTER

5

Crime Scene Examination & Inspection

COMPONENT THREE

"

If the law has made you a witness, remain a man of science. You have no victim to avenge, no guilty or innocent person to convict or save--you must bear witness within the limits of science.

- DR. P.C.H. BROUARDEL

THE CRIME SCENE EXAMINATION & INSPECTION

Inspection of the crime scene or the site of any other important events relating to the allegations in question can be very beneficial to the criminal defense investigator. It is advisable to visit the crime scene or relevant site at the same time of day as the incident in question. The most important rule in crime scene examination is that the scene and all evidence at the scene be examined, processed, and photographed prior to anything being moved. Unfortunately, the criminal defense investigator is often not afforded this luxury. By the time a case is assigned to a criminal defense investigator, the case is usually several days, weeks, or months old. However, criminal defense crime scene examinations are generally focused on the physical layout and critical features of the scene as opposed to the location of evidence. The physical layout of a scene and the dimensions of the scene generally involve fixed objects. Therefore, they generally do not change with time. The purpose of the criminal defense investigators examination of the crime scene is to confirm or dismiss that the testimonial evidence presented corresponds with the critical features of the scene. Considering the criteria of truth discussed in chapter two, the crime scene examination would appear to be a functional example of the correspondence and coherence methods in action.

Crime scenes vary in nature and location such as indoor, outdoor, automobiles, etc. However, specific guidelines apply to the examination and inspection of all scenes. All scenes should be processed utilizing the following guidelines:

1. Observe - do not disturb potential evidence.
2. Record - Accomplish notes, measurements, photographs, and diagrams.
3. Collect - identify and process evidence.
4. Preserve - protect evidence and maintain the chain of custody.

Upon examining the crime scene or relevant sites the criminal defense investigator should accomplish the following tasks:

1. Conduct a cursory examination of the scene to become familiar with the layout and design of the area in question. Record any distinctive observations relative to witness statements.
2. Identify physical changes to the scene which may have occurred since the incident in question.
3. Photograph the crime scene or relevant sites reflecting angles and information on the photograph diagram and photograph log. Based on previous statements and testimony, obtain photographs reflecting the angle and view of witness observations. a video of the crime scene is also recommended.
4. Accomplish a diagram of the scene reflecting major discernible items of physical evidence and critical features of the scene. Measure relevant dimensions and distances accurately. Reflect the location of witnesses based on previous statements or testimony. Recording observations and descriptions of the crime scene

The criminal defense investigator must accomplish detailed and accurate notes as reference. The notes may be used to question witnesses, alternative suspects, victims, or to assist in the preparation of written reports. The notes may also be utilized to refresh the criminal defense investigator's memory in the event court testimony is required. The following guidelines may be followed to take accurate and detailed notes.

1. Print or write notes in legible handwriting utilizing ink.
2. Identify each page of notes with the investigator's name, date, and case number.
3. Utilize clearly understood terms and short phrases.
4. Accomplish accurate and complete notes in order to assist with the preparation of written reports and court testimony.
5. Notes may include memos as reminders to pursue possible leads identified during the crime scene examination.
6. Do not edit or erase your notes. In the event you make a mistake, line out the entry, initial, and rewrite the correct information.

Upon proceeding to a crime scene or relevant site be sure to make note of the time and date of your arrival. Verify the scene as the scene identified within the police reports. Conduct a cursory examination of the scene to become familiar with the layout and design of the area in question. Record any distinctive observations relative to witness statements. The following guide can be utilized to assist the criminal defense investigator with the recording of observations at the crime scene:

1. Describe the crime scene in detail using the common name of items and general location.
   a. Floor, walls, and ceiling.
   b. Entrance/Exits and doors.
   c. Windows, screens, shades, blinds, drapes.
   d. Lighting fixtures and outlets.
   e. Natural lighting conditions.
   f. Appliances and utilities.
   g. Trash cans, ashtrays, and contents.
   h. Furniture, noting condition.
   i. Personal items and clothing.
2. Utilize the 7-step method of description.
   a. Quantity.
   b. Item.
   c. Color.
   d. Type of Construction.
   e. Approximate size.
   f. Identifying features.
   g. Condition.
3. Based on the allegations, reflect the absence of evidence that would be expected to be present at the crime scene. The following items are commonly found at various types of crime scenes dependent upon the allegations and circumstances.
   a. Blood
   b. Saliva
   c. Seminal Stains
   d. Urine
   e. Sweat
   f. Hair
   g. Fingerprints
   h. Footprints

i. Tire Tracks
j. Fabrics
k. Fibers
l. Firearms
m. Knives
n. Gunshot Residue
o. Grease
p. Cigarette Butts
q. Questioned Documents
r. Tool Marks
s. Glass (broken)
t. Narcotics

PHOTOGRAPHING THE CRIME SCENE

"A picture can be worth a thousand words," may or may not be true. However, photography properly performed at the crime scene can be very beneficial to defense counsel. Properly accomplished photographs and a video will supplement notes, diagrams, and written reports. All camera positions should be recorded on the crime scene diagram. It is preferable to note the camera positions on a copy of the crime scene diagram or a secondary version. It is best to keep the camera at eye level, unless a tripod is used. It is very important to maintain perspective when photographing a crime scene. Proper photographic perspective produces the same impression of relative position and size of visible objects as the actual objects do when viewed from a particular point. Any significant distortion in the perspective will reduce, or destroy, its evidentiary value.

An effective criminal defense investigator must have the necessary equipment at his disposal at all times when working in the field. The camera is probably one of the most important items within the criminal defense investigator's inventory. However, the criminal defense investigator will often find himself confronted with a situation which requires only one or two photographs immediately. Therefore, the standard and most widely utilized 35 mm camera becomes somewhat of a problem. The problem usually consists of wasting entire roles of film and waiting at least an hour for emergency developing. With this in mind, the polaroid camera can be a most effective and efficient tool for the criminal defense investigator operating in field conditions. It's simple but effective. The polaroid does not replace the 35 mm as the most effective camera but it does, under certain circumstances, provide an instant alternative. In fact, the 35 mm camera should be used unless field conditions and time limitations dictate otherwise.

The following requirements should be met when accomplishing photography of a Crime Scene:

1. All the approaches to the crime scene.

2. The areas surrounding the crime scene.

3. The interior and exterior of the building.

4. Close-up photographs of the entrances and exits to the crime scene.

5. Overlapping photographs of the crime scene intended to depict the area as a whole, moving in one direction, around the crime scene.

Record the technical data for each photograph in your notes and on a photograph log. Assign each photograph a number within your notes and on the photograph. Describe what each photograph depicts and cite

PHOTOGRAPHIC LOG WORKSHEET

INVESTIGATOR/PHOTOGRAPHER: ______________________________

CASE #: ____________________ CLIENT: ____________________

LOCATION: ______________________________

DATE OF PHOTOGRAPHY: __________ WEATHER CONDITIONS: ____________________

TIME: _______ Began taking crime scene photographs and drawing rough sketch to depict camera positions and distances. All photographs taken at eye level height (") unless otherwise indicated. All interior photographs are taken with the following equipment:

CAMERA TYPE: ____________________ BODY NUMBER: ____________________

LENS FOCAL LENGTH AND LENS SERIAL NUMBER: ______________________________

____

TYPE OF FILM : ____________________ NUMBER OF EXPOSURES: ____________________

ASA: ____________________ FILTRATION: ____________________

F/STOP: ____________________ SHUTTER SPEED: ____________________

FLASH ATTACHMENT: ____________________ FLASH SERIAL #: ____________________

EXPLANATION OF TERMS USED IN **REMARKS**: Camera held in horizontal format, unless otherwise noted. DA - photograph taken from directly above the object; V - camera held in a vertical format; N - normal lens; M - macro lens; WA - wide angle; WO - without ruler; WR - with ruler.

TIME	PHOTO#	TYPE PHOTO	DEPICTING	DISTANCE	REMARKS

the time and date. Record the distance to the focal point. Reflect what type of camera was used and at what height it was held. In addition, state what lens was used and if a flash was used.

ACCOMPLISHING A DIAGRAM OF THE CRIME SCENE

A diagram and photographs of the crime scene and relevant sites can be very valuable to the defense. Properly prepared diagrams may be utilized to develop leads, uncover discrepancies, question witnesses, identify the location of witnesses at the time of the crime, and lock a witness into specific testimony. Diagrams are very valuable sources of information for the criminal defense investigator and defense counsel and should be accomplished properly. A properly prepared diagram and photographs may be used to assist defense counsel at trial and introduced as evidence to familiarize the court with the crime scene and help witnesses orient themselves as they testify.

Diagrams also complement notes and photographs. Diagrams communicate information the way a photograph does, with the added advantage of eliminating unneeded distracting details. There are two types of diagrams or sketches utilized by the criminal defense investigator: rough and smooth. A rough diagram is drawn at the crime scene, reflecting information accurately and is not drawn to scale. However, the rough diagram must reflect distances and dimensions accurately. A smooth diagram is a finished version of the rough diagram, preferably drawn to scale by an experienced draftsman from information obtain by the criminal defense investigator and reflected on the rough diagram.

The following materials are needed to accomplish A rough diagram:

Any kind of paper may be used to accomplish the rough diagram. However, bond or graph paper is best.

1. A pencil.
2. A ruler.
3. A 100 foot measuring tape and measuring wheel.
4. A magnetic compass.
5. A clip board or hardcover notebook.

Several items are considered essential when accomplishing a crime scene diagram. The diagram should include and reflect the major features of the crime scene. In addition, the diagram must be clearly intelligible to the viewer without a detailed study.

The following information should be included and reflected on the diagram:

1. The Investigator's full name and title.
2. The date, time, defendant's name, and case number.
3. The full name of any person assisting the investigator.
4. Address of the crime scene or site.
5. Compass direction.
6. The major items of physical evidence and the critical features of the crime scene.

Measurements reflected on a diagram must be as accurate as possible. An error can introduce doubt questioning the credibility and accuracy of the entire diagram and the criminal defense investigator's ability. Various diagram methods can be utilized to reflect a crime scene. The simplest method to diagram a crime scene is the two-dimensional presentation as viewed from directly above. This method is most commonly used by the criminal defense investigator.

Upon examining indoor and outdoor crime scenes objects and evidence can be located on the two-dimensional diagram by utilizing the coordinate method or triangulation. The coordinate method utilizes the principle of measuring the distance of an object from two fixed points. The measurements of a baseline are determined utilizing a wall or by drawing a line between two fixed points. The object is then Measured from left to right along the baseline to a point at right angles to the object in question.

Triangulation identifies the location of objects by creating a triangle of measurements from a specific point on an object to two fixed points all on the same plane. If mobile items are to be used as reference points, they must first be fixed themselves. Do not measure distances through space and always measure distances along a solid surface. In addition, when triangulating objects, maintain an angle of triangulation between 45 and 90 degrees at all times.

Regular shaped objects are fixed by creating two triangles of measurements. Each originates at opposite points on the object and ends at two fixed points. This method is known as the 2-V method of triangulation. Pliable or odd shaped objects are fixed by creating a single triangle of measurement from the center of mass of the object to fixed points. The longest and widest dimensions of the object must also be measured and reflected on the diagram utilizing this method.

The following is an example of how a properly prepared crime scene diagram can assist defense counsel to impeach witness testimony:

CASE STUDY: ATTEMPTED BURGLARY

According to sworn testimony, at approximately 2 a.m., Witness (A) was in her bedroom and awoke to a rattling noise coming from outside her home. Specifically, adjacent to her spare bedroom window facing her front yard. The spare bedroom is located on the southeast corner of the residence. Witness (A) states that upon hearing the noise in question she got out of bed and looked out of her master bedroom window. According to Witness (A), she observed a tall dark figure, Suspect (B), kneeling adjacent to the spare bedroom window. The husband of Witness (A) departed the master bedroom and turned on the outside porch light via a light switch inside the foyer area adjacent to the front door. According To Witness (A), the light startled the Suspect (B), causing him to pause, providing Witness (A) with an opportunity to "clearly observe Suspect (B)", describing him as "a tall white male, wearing loose fitting clothing." Subsequently, Suspect (B) ran south into the darkness. The husband of Witness (A) did not observe the suspect. Approximately 45 minutes later police apprehended the defendant walking approximately one mile from the residence in question. The defendant, a 22 year old white male, 6 feet, 185 pounds, wearing long black shorts and a large blue T-Shirt, was questioned by police and asked to participate in a line-up. The defendant complied with the request. Subsequently, Witness (A) identified the defendant from a line-up as the suspect who attempted to gain entry into her home. The defendant was arrested and charged with attempted burglary of a dwelling.
Investigative Findings: Criminal Defense Investigators proceeded to the area in question and conducted an examination of the crime scene. A two dimensional diagram of the crime scene was accomplished reflecting all major features of the scene as well as accurate measurements (Refer to Diagram). Photographs of the crime scene and photographs reflecting the angle of observation by Witness (A) were also accomplished to accompany the diagram. Close examination of the crime scene, diagram, and photographs revealed that the testimony of Witness (A), regarding her observations of the Suspect (B), is improbable. Based on the physical design of the residence and sworn testimony, it would appear to be impossible for witness (A) to observe the

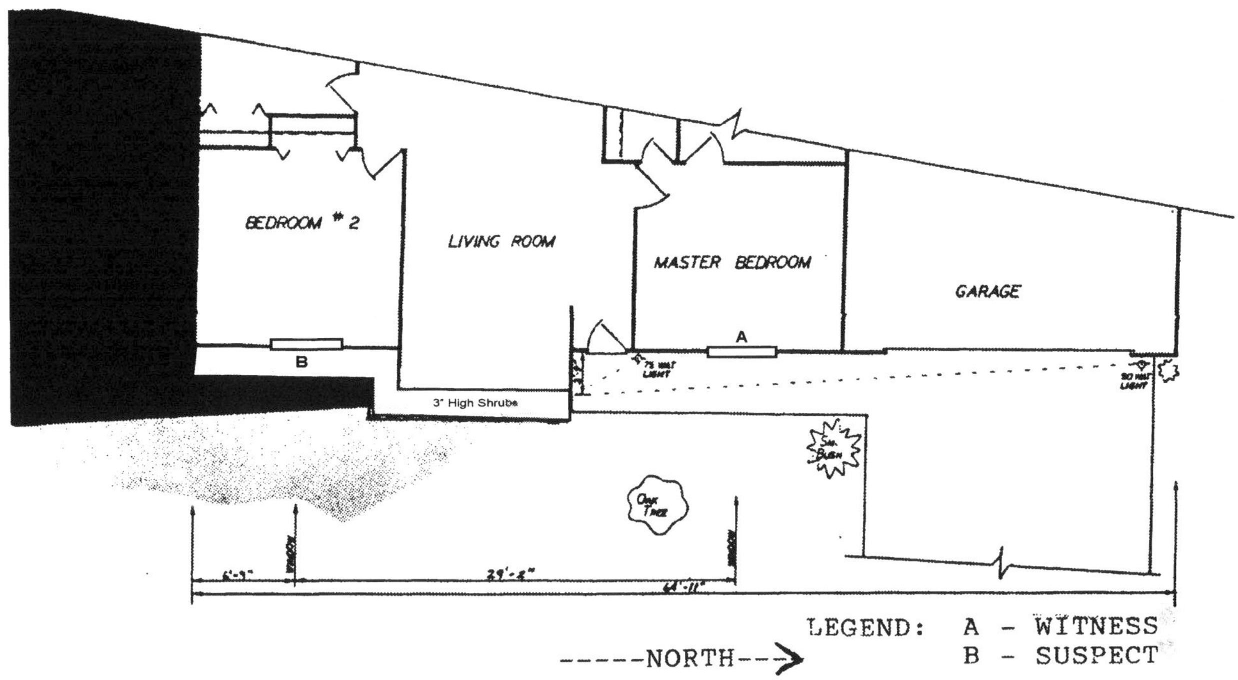

CRIME SCENE DIAGRAM

Suspect (B) from her master bedroom window as he attempted to gain entry via the spare bedroom window. As reflected on the diagram, the ability of Witness (A) to observe activity adjacent to the spare bedroom window would be obstructed by a portion of the house which extends out 2 feet 9 inches. This extension would also obstruct the ability of the 75 watt exterior light to illuminate the area adjacent to the spare bedroom window. In addition, Witness (A) stated that she "clearly observed" the suspect, from a distance of 29 ft 2 inches, as he was kneeling adjacent to the spare bedroom window. The diagram also reflects a 3 ft high hedge around the house which could have obstructed the observations of Witness (A). Therefore, the crime scene examination, diagram, and photographs significantly raise the issue of reasonable doubt and question the credibility of the eye witness and the identification line-up implicating the defendant.

Although the criminal defense investigator will rarely encounter significant physical or trace evidence at the crime scene, he should be prepared when confronted with potential evidence. The following is an example of such a situation.

CASE STUDY: HOMICIDE/EUTHANASIA

A 71 year old man became the subject of a national spotlight when according to police he smothered his wife of 48 years as she lay dying of cancer. The question as to whether or not the defendant loved his wife or not was not a focus of the police investigation. The question was whether or not his wife wished to die.

The defendant claimed that his act was one of love and mercy. The defendant's 68 year old wife had been diagnosed with cancer approximately six months earlier. Unfortunately, surgery and treatment were unable to stop the spread of cancer. Therefore, bedridden and in pain, the defendant and nurses could only administer medicine to reduce the pain. According to medical experts, at the time of her death the victim was within days if not hours of death. On the last day of her life the victim was in extreme pain and unable to move or speak. Moments before his wife's death, the defendant asked the grief counselor to wait in the study because he wished to be alone with his wife. The counselor reported that she was watching television when she heard a muffled cry from the bedroom. She knocked on the door and asked the defendant what happened. The defendant replied that everything was fine. However, moments later the counselor heard another cry and burst into the room to find the defendant with what police describe as a piece of "bubble wrap" over the victim's face. The counselor attempted to stop the defendant but he grabbed her arm and pulled her from the room telling her to leave. Subsequently, the counselor called 911 resulting in a police response within three minutes. When police arrived the victim was dead and the defendant was arrested for murder.

Immediately following the defendant's arrest, the police initiated a crime scene examination of the defendant's and victim's home. Based upon police reports it would appear that the crime scene examination was conducted thoroughly and followed accepted procedures. Examination and search of the crime scene by police uncovered what police claimed to be the instrument of death. According to police, the defendant utilized a piece of "bubble wrap" plastic to smother the victim. In retrospect, identification of the instrument of death appears to be based upon a vague description by the grief counselor and the fact that the "bubble wrap" was the only plastic found by crime scene detective during their search of the home. The police were under great pressure to locate the instrument of death and appeared to have stopped at the first sign of a possible hit. The "bubble wrap" was found among boxes in the study closet, the same room where the grief counselor had been waiting. The police claimed that they conducted a complete search of the entire home.

However, the defendant claimed that the police were mistaken and that the "bubble wrap" was not the instrument of death. According to the defendant, he had promised his wife months earlier that he would not allow her to die in pain. Up until moments before her death he had been able to control his wife's pain with morphine. But hours before her death the pain became too great to control. To add to the frustration, the nurse hired to assist his wife left him alone sending only an untrained volunteer grief counselor. Two days prior to his wife's death, the defendant prepared a plastic bag designed to fit over one's head and tighten around the neck utilizing a plastic band. The defendant's intent was that of a mercy killing for his bedridden wife and a suicide for himself. The police claimed that they discovered no evidence to support he intended to commit suicide. During his wife's last moments he could no longer watch as she lay whimpering in agonizing pain. Subsequently, he escorted the grief counselor out of the room and then placed the plastic bag over his wife's head and watched her slowly pass away. When police arrived they restrained the defendant and sat him on the couch in the living room as they searched the home. It is at this time, in the presence and under the supervision of a detective, that the defendant states he removed the plastic bag from his front pocket and placed it under the cushion of the couch as the detective used the telephone.

Obviously it was important to verify the defendant's statement in order to corroborate his version of the events in question. Therefore, defense counsel directed a private investigator to proceed to the crime scene and search for the suspected instrument of death as well as conduct a defense examination of the crime scene. The defense investigator verified that the police released the crime scene and that entry had not been gained by other parties. A systematic examination of the scene was accomplished. Initially, upon lifting the seat cushion in question, from back to front, no plastic bag was discovered. The seat cushion was then completely removed from the couch a plastic bag similar in design to the one described by the defendant. The bag was found at the front of the cushion consistent with the actions as described by the defendant. The plastic bag was photographed but not removed or disturbed any further. It should also be noted that additional evidence was recovered at the scene including medical records and documents supporting the defendant's position. Pursuant to the direction of defense counsel, the police were notified and responded to recover the evidence.

The police arrived on the scene accompanied by the detective responsible for the initial search. The detective immediately demonstrated a suspicious and arrogant attitude questioning not only the credibility of the evidence discovered but the credibility of the defense investigator and defense counsel. The defense investigator overheard the detective telling the other officer's that he himself searched the couch initially and no plastic bag was present. Based upon the advice of the detective the plastic bag was recovered but dismissed as potential evidence. It would appear that the detective's ego was severely bruised because he failed to uncover the instrument of death during his original search. He was willing to place his own interests above the interest of justice. Apparently, the truth did not coincide with description of the incident developed by police. The confusing part is that the plastic bag did not necessarily help the defendant considering it provided evidence that the act was not a last minute act of desperation but planned two days prior to the death.

Unfortunately, the evidence was never evaluated nor was the truth officially decided by a jury. Shortly after bonding out of the county jail, the defendant committed suicide in his home.

BLOODSTAIN PATTERN ANALYSIS AND DETECTION

The following section was provided by Brad A. Perron, Criminalist, Forensic Consultant

Criminal courts across the nation accept the use of Bloodstain Pattern Analysis, also known as Blood Spatter Analysis, as an area of forensic science which is based on the laws of physics (ballistics) and mathematics. Bloodstain Pattern Analysis is a scientific discipline that involves identification, comparison, examination, and evaluation of the physical evidence of bloodstains.

Examination of evidence at the crime scene, and recovered from the scene of any event sufficiently violent to have resulted in bloodshed, should include a detailed study of all detectable bloodstains. Observations made during such a study can often provide sufficient information to reconstruct the conditions at the moment of bloodshed. The results of the study may allow conclusions to be reached in answering vital questions regarding the details of the act itself. These answers should assist in resolving the matter regarding the actions of the perpetrator(s) and the victim(s).

The study of the bloodstains is beneficial in many aspects. The origin of bloodshed may be established by determining the directionality of the stain and the angle at which blood impacted the surface. The size and shape of the stain can also be used to help determine the origin of bloodshed. Ascertaining the movement of persons and/or objects following the moment of bloodshed can sometimes provide more insight than those related to the moment of bloodshed. Blood transferred from one object to another often relates to the actions of a perpetrator during and after the crime is committed. Flow patterns can be identified and used to determine if a body was moved or was moving during or after bloodshed. Recognition of the resulting stain patterns can be extremely beneficial to the reconstruction of the chain of events that occurred.

The manner of injury is a crucial aspect of all violent crimes. Determining the force of impact and distance traveled can be used to determine blood velocity, which in turn relates to the mechanism of force. Medium velocity impact spatter patterns are commonly associated with blunt force trauma injuries. High velocity impact spatter is associated with gunshots or explosions. The blood spatter pattern evidence can be coupled with evidence procured by the medical examiner or hospital staff.

A trained bloodstain pattern analyst can determine important facts regarding incidents involving bloodshed, such as:

- if an apparent suicide is genuine or staged
- whether bloodstains on a suspect can place him in close proximity of the victim at the time of bloodshed
- whether bloodstains on an individual's clothing or person are the result of spatter or of attempts to give assistance to a victim
- the direction of the victim's movements and/or suspect's movements

- the minimum number of blows, punctures, or gunshots inflicted on a victim

- the approximate amount of force involved in an assault

The following is an example of how an effective inspection of the law enforcement crime scene report should not overlook the obvious in search of the obscure:

CASE STUDY: HOMICIDE/2ND DEGREE MURDER

Defense investigators will often find themselves spending long hours in social wastelands investigating some of the most unconscionable acts of random violence. Such areas are responsible for a steady flow of interesting and challenging cases. Needless to say, business will steadily increase with the crime rate. The criminal defense investigator is presented with the opportunity to investigate a number of interesting cases for the defense involving creative defense angles and solid alternative suspects. Although not the most gruesome, violent, or tragic by any means, the following case is a fine example of an effective criminal defense investigation focused upon the crime scene. The crime in question is a homicide, a stabbing to be specific. The case is interesting because it involves modern forensic techniques and a little dose of good old fashioned deductive reasoning.

Defense Counsel motioned the court to appoint a private investigator to investigate the incident on behalf of his indigent client. The client, a young African American female, in her early thirties, with a non-violent criminal record, was charged with 2nd Degree Murder. The stabbing occurred at her home, a small bungalow, conveniently located in an area known as the combat zone. The neighborhood, a run down heavily populated side street, set the stage for violent crime's latest episode. Stereotypical gang member types litter the street corners, dressed in the appropriate colors signifying their position and status in the community. Pumping out their urban poetry in maximum decibels, the self proclaimed urban ambassadors define their territory, as well as provide a visual message to unwelcome visitors. As in all high crime areas, unfortunate families are forced to live amid the violence, watching their small children play innocently in the streets, and for some eventually to grow to take their place in the urban social clubs littering the very same streets. A defense investigator travels within the combat zone for the most part hassle free, with a few exceptions of course, but that's another story.

The facts of this case were very clear. According to the prosecution's only eye witness, the defendant and the victim, her live-in boyfriend, were engaged in a heated argument in the living room of their residence. According to police reports, based on the testimony of an eye witness, the argument became physical with the victim allegedly pushing the defendant, resulting in the defendant brandishing a knife and subsequently stabbing the victim through the heart, resulting in his death. The only eye witness, also an African American female in her thirties, stated that the stabbing occurred in the living room near the front door. According to the eye witness, "blood was flowing from the victim's chest onto the carpeted floor of the living room and he dragged his hands through the blood as he crawled to and out the front door," to his final resting place on the front porch. Open and shut case, right? Wrong. As you will soon see the open and shut murder case took an interesting turn.

Not surprisingly, initial interview of the defendant revealed that her account of the events in question differed in that she stated the victim arrived at her front door already stabbed and bleeding. Of course, the defendant, was adamant and insisted that she was not guilty. Initially, the attitude of the defense investigator was "of course not, you're not guilty, he stabbed himself." Apathy is definitely a professional hazard when it comes to criminal defense investigation. Sometimes it's very hard not to be cynical. As the interview progressed, gut feelings and ten years of experience told the defense investigator that she just might be telling the truth. The defendant refused generous plea bargains and insisted on going to trial. Being a professional, the defense investigator promised the defendant and her attorney that the prosecution's case would be scrutinized.

The prosecution's case rested heavily upon the testimony of an eye witness, the only eye witness. The first step was to identify the possibility of a motivation behind the eye witness's testimony. Specifically, the eye witness's motivation to lie. Investigation revealed that the prosecution's eye witness had an ongoing rivalry with the defendant because of romantic interests. She also had a violent temper and a reputation for violence. A background investigation revealed that the reputation for violence was backed up by an interesting criminal record. A record consisting of an obviously significant stabbing conviction. Furthermore, the eye witness was unable to provide a plausible reason for being at the residence just as the defendant allegedly stabbed the victim to death in the heart. Thorough investigation, as well as a complete canvass of the neighborhood, was unable to uncover any evidence or witnesses to corroborate the defendant's story. No evidence or witnesses were uncovered supporting the prosecution's witness either. However, the lack of cooperating witnesses in the combat zone is almost a given. This case was coming down to the defendant's word against the witness's word. Often, in the absence of favorable evidence, the defense investigation will uncover additional evidence incriminating the defendant. The defense attorney will in turn use this evidence to convince the defendant that a plea bargain would be a bargain indeed. However, this was not the case. Furthermore, newly uncovered testimonial evidence was not going to play a part in this case. No surprise defense witnesses were going to dramatically appear at the last moment to implicate the alternative suspect.

It was time to turn attention to the physical evidence. The physical evidence at first glance appeared to be very clear. No smoking gun, but the prosecution had a crime, a body, a witness, and a suspect. Review of the autopsy report was clear. The victim died as a result of a stab wound to the heart. No help there. The murder weapon was never found, therefore, never linked to the defendant. A little help, but alone it wasn't much. The next step was an investigative review of the crime scene examination, specifically the crime scene report, diagram, and photographs. Again, the crime scene report was standard. A crime scene and a body. Initially, the report and photographs appeared to reflect the murder as it was described by both the defendant and the witness. However, further scrutiny of the photographs revealed that something was missing. There was a crime scene and a body. Specifically, the victim of a stab wound to the heart. The problem immediately became very clear. Although the front porch and walkway, the final resting place of the body, reflected a large amount of blood, the interior of the residence, just inside the door, where the stabbing allegedly occurred did not. Again, the eye witness stated that the stabbing occurred in the living room near the front door. According to the eye witness, "blood was flowing from the victim's chest onto the carpeted floor of the living room and he dragged his hands through the blood as he crawled to and out the front door." The eye witness's account of the stabbing would indicate a significant presence of blood evidence at the crime scene. However, according to the crime scene report and the photographs, this was not the case. This latest development was brought to the attention of defense counsel. The apparent lack of blood at the crime scene, as well as the eye witness's prior stabbing conviction prompted defense counsel to question the credibility and motivation of her testimony.

Based on these facts, It was decided to examine the crime scene utilizing the services of a forensic investigator and criminalist. Specifically, a forensic biologist trained in the areas of blood detection and the significance of blood stain evidence. Presumptive blood testing techniques were conducted utilizing luminol and phenolphthalein. The living room as well as the carpeted area in front of the door tested negative for the presence of blood. This was a major break in the case. The lack of evidence not only supported the defendant's version but obviously more than questioned the credibility of the prosecution's only eye witness. To sum it up, physical evidence or the lack of it had been uncovered supporting the defendant's innocence. How accurate are the blood detection tests? According to the forensic biologist, "the sensitivity of the luminol test is up to one part per million dilution." In other words, if a bath tub was filled with water to the rim and a drop of blood was added to the water, the luminol would detect the presence of blood. Therefore, attempts to wash away the blood would only dilute the blood to points where it would not be visible to the naked eye but would still be detected. In addition, attempts to remove the blood utilizing bleaching agents would reveal such attempts to conceal the blood evidence. No evidence of bleaching agents was discovered.

The lack of physical evidence detected by forensic investigation directly contradicted the testimony of the prosecution's eye witness. In fact, the lack of blood evidence within the house in conjunction with the presence of blood outside the door and on the walkway not only supported the defendant's innocence, but implicated the prosecution's witness as well. Based on forensic results, as well as the eye witnesses motivation to lie and prior record, defense counsel was able to effectively question her credibility. The prosecution's eye witness testimony was determined to be significantly flawed. Aggressive painstaking investigation and the use of simple deductive reasoning effectively identified "reasonable doubt." Both the prosecution and the defense were unwilling to play the odds at trial. Subsequently, the defendant accepted a plea offer reducing the charges to manslaughter, resulting in 1 year of community control and 2 years probation and no jail time. The prosecution's witness was never prosecuted or pursued as an alternative suspect.

THE TECHNOLOGY OF DNA FINGERPRINTING

The development of DNA technology has raised an interesting issue for the criminal justice system. Specific DNA testing identified as RFLP and PCR as techniques for confirming or excluding the source of a sample of body fluid or tissue have become commonplace. However, it remains common for lay persons and professionals to confuse DNA testing as a "blood type test". DNA is not just found in blood. DNA is located in the nucleus of every cell in the body, white blood cells, tissue cells, bone cells, hair root cells, etc. DNA is an abbreviation for deoxyribosenucleic acid, a molecule in the shape of a double helix, consisting of nitrogenous base pairs held together with hydrogen bonds. DNA is what defines an individual. An individual's DNA determines every single detail about a human being such as eye color. It also determines the shape and size of your eyes and the need for corrective lenses.

In criminal cases DNA technology would appear to be a more effective means of excluding a suspect than to confirm and positively identify one. The reason is that if there is not a match, there is no debate, no arguing over databases, techniques, or size of sample. The samples are simply determined to be different. Unfortunately, the criminal justice system does not always operate with such efficiency.

Kerry Kotler was arrested and convicted of rape charges in 1981. In 1992, DNA tests performed on his blood and semen evidence recovered from the victim did not produce a match. After 11 years in prison, the charges were dropped and Kotler was freed. However, it should be noted that Kotler's defense team was forced to wage an uphill battle just to convince the prosecution to agree to performing a DNA test. The Suffolk County New York District Attorney opposed Kotler's appeals for two years. The District Attorney, unconvinced of Kotler's innocence, suggested that the samples were contaminated in the laboratory. The prosecution is often very enthusiastic utilizing DNA technology to convict defendants. Unfortunately, the enthusiasm appears to wane when used to exclude a defendant.

DNA - A BRIEF HISTORY

DNA Fingerprinting was developed by Sir Alec Jeffreys, a geneticist at the University of Leicester in England in the early 1980's. DNA Fingerprinting was first used in a rape/murder case of a seventeen year old in England. A seventeen year old boy confessed to the crime, but was cleared using DNA Fingerprinting. His DNA did not match that of the perpetrator's DNA. Jeffreys and his staff then took blood samples from all the adult males that lived in the area to try and find the actual perpetrator. One man, Colin Pitchfork, tried to pay a friend to submit to the blood test for him. Pitchfork's attempt to bypass the test was discovered and his blood was tested. The DNA Fingerprint of Pitchfork matched that of the DNA sample taken from sperm found in the victim's body. Pitchfork was convicted of the crime and sentenced to life in prison.

The first case in which DNA profiling evidence was admitted into court in the United States occurred in Florida in 1987. Tommie Lee Andrews was tried for rape and the victim was unable to identify her assailant. This Orlando case had Lifecodes Laboratory comparing the DNA of Andrews with the DNA of sperm found at the crime scene. The conclusion was that the two samples matched and Andrews received a sentence of 78 years in prison. The first capital case was a 1988 Florida case. Randall Scott Jones was tried for the murder of a man and woman and the after death rape of the woman in Putnam County. Cellmark Diagnostics matched the blood sample taken from Jones with the sperm sample extracted from the woman's body. Jones received the death penalty after the jury deliberated for only 12 minutes.

WHAT IS DNA?

1. DNA is the chemical substance that makes up our chromosomes and controls information that determines a person's individual characteristics; such as eye, hair, and skin color.

2. DNA is different for every individual except for identical twins.

3. DNA is found in all cellular material; white blood cells, tissue cells, bone cells, hair root cells, and spermatozoa.

4. One half of an individual's DNA (chromosomes) comes from a person's father, the other half from the person's mother.

5. DNA is a double stranded macromolecule. The double strand is actually coiled around a central axis. The illustration to the left shows a model of a portion of DNA straightened out from around the axis.

6. The DNA strands are chemically made up of four basic building blocks, called nucleotides, which are represented by the letters A (adenine), G (guanine), C (cytosine), and T (thymine). The bonding of the nucleotide pairs is specific in that only A-T and G-C pairs are allowed. These nucleotides are linked in a chain-like sequence, and their order can vary to provide an almost infinite number of possible arrangements.

7. The four nucleotides and their sequence in the DNA makes up the letters of the genetic code. A complete strand of human DNA stores all the information making up the the "human genome." A complete strand of DNA is coiled inside all human cells and would be six feet long if straightened out.

8. There are approximately 3 billion nucleotide pairs in the entire human genetic code. Each pair represents a "rung" on the twisted ladder of the DNA model.

9. The genetic code for one person, if written out, would take up enough space to fill about a hundred and twenty five Manhattan telephone directories.

10. In specific regions on a DNA strand, each person has a unique sequence of building block nucleotides. This in an important factor used in DNA Fingerprinting.

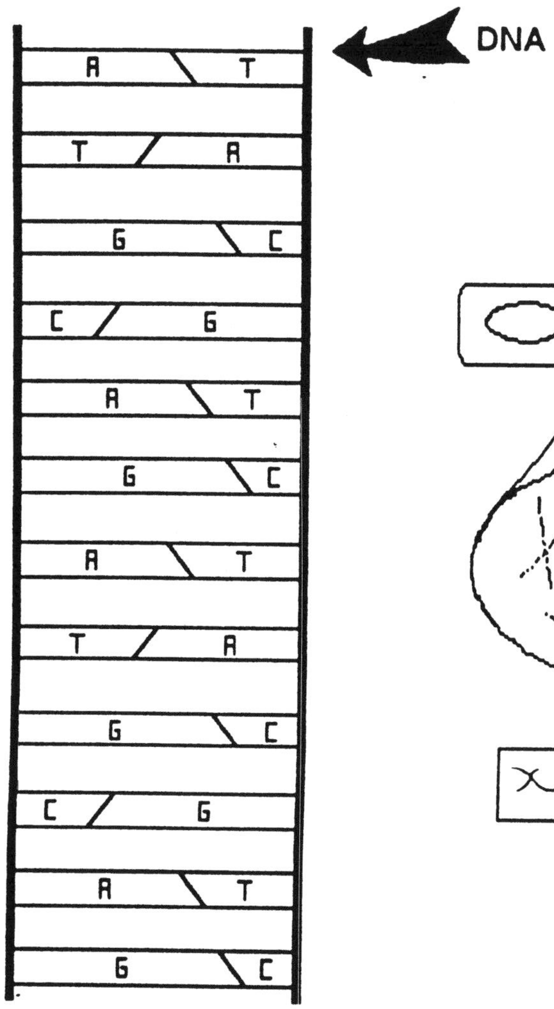
DNA
A T
T A
G C
C G
A T
G C
A T
T A
G C
C G
A T
G C

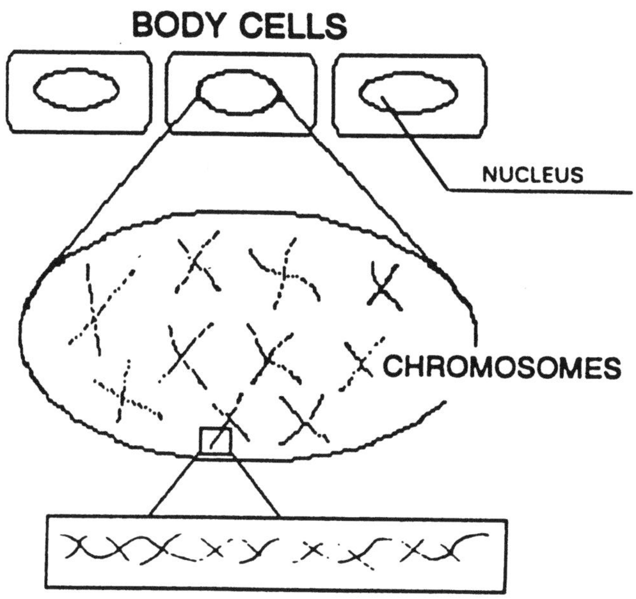
BODY CELLS
NUCLEUS
CHROMOSOMES

CHAPTER

6

The Alleged Victim & Witness Background Investigation

COMPONENT FOUR

"

Either a good or a bad reputation outruns and gets before people wherever they go.

-LORD CHESTERFIELD

The police reports will generally list the name of the victim and witnesses that the prosecution may call to testify against the defendant. Generally, by law, in answer to a demand for discovery filed by the defense, the prosecution is required to provide a list of all witnesses who may have information regarding the case. However, during the initial stages of the criminal defense investigation, the criminal defense investigator may not have the answer to demand for discovery listing the prosecution witnesses. Therefore, the criminal defense investigator may have to rely on his review of the police reports and initial interview of the defendant to identify potential prosecution witnesses.

A background investigation of the prosecution witnesses as well as the defense witnesses can be very beneficial to defense counsel. Negative information uncovered by the defense can be used to impeach the prosecution witnesses, questioning their credibility as witnesses. In addition, a background investigation of defense witnesses can alert defense counsel to any credibility questions or potential impeachment of defense witnesses. The background investigation can also provide insight regarding the criteria of truth utilized by a witness based upon past life experiences. The criminal defense investigator should attempt to gather all available information regarding the witnesses to be interviewed. Information such as arrest and conviction records, education, character, reputation, associates, habits, and all other available records should be pursued.

The criminal defense invesigator should develop a dossier on each witness which can be submitted to defense counsel upon completion. In addition to conventional public records research, commercial databases can identify social security numbers, dates of birth, aliases, prior addresses, known associates, business associations, licensing, assets, and a multitude of additional information regarding an individual. Many leads can be developed from this information. Potential fruad indicators such as the use of an alias or more than one social security number may be uncovered accessing such sources of information.

There is a great deal of information documented within public records that can be accessed by the criminal defense investigator. Information on the federal, state, county, and municipal levels can provide valuable information and additional leads. The following is a list of locations where records may be accessed dependent upon local and state laws.

1. Federal Criminal History Records.
2. Federal Court Civil Records.
3. Other Federal Agencies.
4. State Criminal Records
5. State Agency Records
6. Motor Vehicle Records maintained by the state and accessible in each county courthouse.
7. County Criminal Records located within the courthouse of each county.
8. Civil court records, filed within the courthouse of each county reflecting civil law suits.
9. Marriage records, divorce files, and domestic violence injunctions filed within the Family Division of each county courthouse.
10. Municipal and County Agency Records.
11. Local Law Enforcement Records

12. On-line services, data bases, and information brokers. The public library maintains several data bases accessing information on local and national levels.

When reviewing records and files, it is very important to read the documents very carefully. Again, as earlier discussed, the average person tends to view documents, retaining little, if any specifics. Therefore, it is important to read the entire document, noting any significant information or possible leads.

In addition, the criminal defense investigator may be denied access to information by specific agencies. With this in mind, sources or connections at the following agencies may by of great assistance:

1. Federal law enforcement agencies.
2. State and local law enforcement agencies.
3. United States Armed Forces.
4. The Internal Revenue Service.
5. Department of Corrections.
6. Federal agencies and departments.
7. State and local government.
8. Public utilities.
9. Private business and community organizations.
10. Family and friends of the subject.
11. Former employers and or business contacts.
12. Fellow employees.

The criminal defense investigator should also keep in mind that an individual's reputation within the community is not only recorded in the form of documentary evidence. The records uncovered will more than likely identifiy potential witnesses who can provide testimony regarding an individual's reputation. For example, a person victimized by the subject of the background investigation in a previous crime may be able to testify regarding the subject's reputation for honesty or violence based upon personal experience and observations. Therefore, the criminal defense investigator must scrutinize records very carefully and consider the pursuit of potential witnesses as sources of impeachment information as well.

The following are examples of how an effective background investigation can provide insight into the character and credibility of a witness or alleged victim.

CASE STUDY: SEXUAL BATTERY

Two men accused of raping a pregnant woman in St. Lucie County Florida were arrested and charged with sexual battery, kidnapping, and aggravated battery. The men were held in the county jail with the bond set at $ 150,000 each. According to police reports, the alleged victim was kidnapped by the two men at approximately 1 a.m. on a main highway in front of a local motel. The threesome allegedly drove to an abandoned grove where she was reportedly raped by the men. After having sex, the three drove into the adjacent county where they encountered a deputy sheriff on the side of the road directing traffic because of an automobile accident. At this time the woman yelled to the deputy that the men had kidnapped and raped her. The two men were subsequently arrested.

The defendants retained the services of defense counsel, who immediately ordered a complete investigation into the matter. A private investigator was hired to conduct the investigation for the defense. Preliminary investigative results were uncovered contradicting the alleged victim's statements. Specifically, statements from witnesses revealed that she willfully departed with the defendants in front of a motel frequented by prostitutes. She claimed to police that she was forced to leave with the them. This information was presented to the prosecution. Subsequently, the defendants' bonds were reduced to $ 10,000 each. the defendants were able to make bond and were released.

The defense Investigation intensified resulting in the discovery that the alleged victim had a documented history of prostitution and a tendency to claim rape when payment was not rendered. In fact, according to court records, at the time of the incident, the woman was on probation for a conviction for Solicitation of Prostitution. The defendants never denied having sex with the woman but denied forcing her to engage in the sexual activity. According to defense counsel, "My clients may have used poor judgement that night, but they didn't kidnap or rape anybody." Subsequently all charges against the defendants were dropped. The background investigation uncovered significant evidence to impeach the credibility of the alleged victim and convince the prosecution that pursuit of the charges would not be in the best interest of justice.

CASE STUDY: HOMICIDE/1ST DEGREE MURDER

A victim of circumstance or a cold blooded killer? The defendant, a 17 year old boy, was charged with the beating death of an 80 year old woman. The police were called to the scene of the crime by the father of the defendant. Upon arrival, the police found the victim lying on the couch of her living room covered with blood. Her face was beaten beyond recognition and her blood stained the furniture, floor, and walls from what appeared to be a relentless attack on the fragile woman. The defendant was found covered with the victim's blood. He denied responsibility for the murder and inisted he found the victim dead.

The defendant, a habitual drug user, spent the previous year in a perpetual high. He degenerated into the typcial drug user; unemployed, living at home or on the street, stealing from family and friends, and thinking only of his next fix. His family, a religious and hard working clan, had enough when they learned he and a female employee of their convenience store were stealing from the store to support a mutual drug habit. A large amount of cash was taken resulting in the defendant's father confronting him with little room for denial. The defendant admitted that he and the female employee took the funds in order to buy drugs. The father informed his son that they would proceed to the woman's home to retrieve the stolen money. Subsequentely, they drove to her home where she resided with her boyfriend and his 80 year old grandmother. The defendant entered the home alone while his father waited in the car. According to the defendant, he approached the house and found the door wide open. Having been to the home several times he knew that the woman's boyfriend was working. Upon entering the dwelling he expected to find his co-conspirator or her boyfriend's grandmother. He claims that he found the victim on the couch unconscious and covered with blood. On the floor adjacent to her were several empty boxes and an old rifle. He also claims that he attempted to assist her providing an explanation for being covered with her blood. Realizing that she was severely injured he exited the home with the rifle and attempted to gain the assistance of his father. Upon seing his son covered with blood with a rifle in his hand he angrily instructed him to return the rifle where he found it and get into the car at once. They immediately departed the scene and returned to their home only minutes away. Upon returning home the defendant's father telephoned 911 and reported the discovery.

Prior to the arrival of police the verbal exchange between father and son escalated. The heated exchange resulted in the defendant panicking and fleeing his home covered with blood. It did not take long for the police to issue an all points bulletin for the defendant's arrest. A couple of hours passed resulting in the apprehension of the defendant. He was strung out on drugs, covered with blood, and desperate. However, he had little to say and did not admit to killing the victim or being responsible for it in any way. The set of facts set forth would appear to be compelling and supportive of the defendant's innocence. However, further investigation by the police resulted in a confusing and complex case. A search of the defendant's home discovered several handguns hidden on the property outside the home. According to the defendant's alleged co-conspirator, the handguns had been stolen from the victim's home during what the police described as a burglary/homicide. The handguns were allegedly kept in boxes underneath the couch along with an antique rifle.

The plot thickened when the defendant's co-conspirator, who will be referred to hereafter as "Jane", denied his allegations. She claimed that he alone was responsible for the theft at his parent's store and probably entered her home with the intent of commiting a burglary to support his habit. She stated that the defendant had visited the home several times and knew where the guns were kept. Although she admitted to having smoked marijuana with the defendant she denied any further involvement with him. The police disregarded the set of facts presented by the defendant's father and opted to charge the defendant with 1st degree murder. The family immediately hired an attorney who in turn retained the services of a private investigator specializing in criminal defense investigations. The case against the defendant was very compelling. The prosecution aggresively and effectively attacked the credibility of the defendant's father. What appeared to be compelling evidence for the defense evolved into uncorraborated and desperate testimony motivated by a father's love for his son. Therefore, the defense initiated an aggressive and comprehensive investigation to uncover evidence to support the defendant's position and the testimony of his father. A team of experienced criminal defense investigators and forensic experts was assembled to carry out the task.

The investigative approach was initiated utilizing the component method of criminal defense investigation as a guide. An investigative review of the prosecution's case not only provided the investigative team with superior knowledge and compelling leads but it also identified volumes of discrepencies and inconsistencies internal to the case itself. Unfortunately, an interview with the defendant was of little assistance. The defendant's inability to recall events and communicate effectively due to prolonged use of illegal drugs rendered him useless to his own defense. An inspection and examination of the crime scene was conducted but provided little insight. An expert in blood stain interpretation was brought into the case as a consultant and provided an alternative opinion regarding the blood stain patterns found at the scene and on the defendant's clothing. The expert retained by the defense determined that the blood found on the defendant's clothing was the result of transfer as opposed to spatter. Such a conclusion supported the defendant's claim that he attempted to provide assistance to the victim. However, the prosecution's expert differed in his opinion stating that although transfer patterns were present, he also found very minute evidence of medium velocity spatter which was consistent with blunt force trauma injuries. A jury would have to determine which expert was more credible.

The defense team focused its attention upon the prosecution's key witness. Jane represented the very foundation of the prosecution's case. Therefore, defense investigators initiated an extensive background investigation regarding her reputation for truthfullness and violence within the community. The background investigation consisted of complete records checks and the identification and interview of any and all persons knowing her or known to associate with her. The background investigation unearthed interesting information. A records check revealed that although Jane's criminal record was limited it did reflect an arrest regarding the theft and fraudulent use of stolen credit cards. However, the charges were dropped. It is true that the arrest provided insight regarding her reputation for honesty but it also provide much more. The credit cards in question were stolen from the victim approximately three months prior to her death while Jane lived in her home. Further investigation revealed that Jane began dating the victim's grandson approximately six months prior to her death. It was also learned that the victim did not care for Jane. Her grandson, a confirmed alcoholic, ignored her and allowed Jane to move in with them. Neighbors, family, and friends of the victim provided testimony supporting that the vitim often complained of Jane's lifestyle and wanted her out of the house. They also related that Jane munipulated the victim's grandson and subsequentely began to control the victim's life.

Witnesses also provided testimony regarding Jane's knowledge that in the event the victim were to die her grandson would inherit the house and property. Slowly but surely the defense team began to develop Jane as an alternative suspect. Motive, means, and opportunity were being identified, supported, and corroborated.

The defense investigators continued the assault pursing every lead and interviewing all potential witnesses. The investigation revealed that only two days prior to the incident, Jane was with the defendant engaged in what was described by witnesses as an "all night party of drugs and sex". The most compelling part of the night in question was that three independent witnesses related that Jane and the defendant were in possession of several handguns and an antique rifle. According to witnesses, they were attempting to sell the guns in order to buy drugs. The statements provided by witnesses appeared to provide a possible explanation for the guns being hidden outside the defendant's home. The witnesses who observed the attempt to sell the guns were also subject to backround investigations. At this point the case took another interesting turn. The investigation began to develop two additional alternative suspects. The suspects, both men, had extensive criminal records, knew Jane, and had been in her home. They were also aware of the guns and where they were kept. An extensive background investigation into one of the suspects revealed that his criminal record included several acts of violence and an attempted murder charge, a murder for hire to be exact. The charges alleged that while in prison he was hired to kill another inmate. The charges were dropped because of lack of sufficient evidence but the victim was found and provided a statement supporting the allegations. The second alternative suspect, like the defendant, was an extensive drug user. He also was familiar with Jane and was alleged to have been in the victim's home several times. The compelling evidence incriminating him came in the form of a former girlfiend stating he confessed to the crime. She contacted the defense stating the police were informed but had botched an attempt to have the alternative suspect confess while she wore a wire. Apparentely, during the attempted sting operation he became suspicious and discovered the wire. As time wore on the case became more and more complex. Defense counsel was faced with a serious dillema: several compelling defenses to choose from including three alternative suspects.

The criminal defense investigators engaged in a comprehensive and systematic investigation which left no stone unturned. The invesitgation was a perfect example of how a well planned investigation following proven guidelines and procedures can develop compelling evidence. It should be noted that the criminal defense investigators were fortunate to have been provided with the resources to pursue such a diligent and effective investigation. The case went to trial and the evidence and arguments presented by the prosecution and defense were compelling as well as overwhelming. It is possible that too much information was presented. The first trial resulted in a mistrial. The second lasted several weeks and resulted in as many interesting turns and surprises as in the defense investigation. However, as in all trials one can never forecast what the end result will be. A jury found the defendant guilty of 1st degree murder. It should be noted that the evidence uncovered by the defense investigation may have left an impression on the prosecution. They opted not to pursue the death penalty and the defendant was sentenced to 40 years in prison, a prime example of how a verdict is not always an accurate representation of an effective and successful investigation.

CHAPTER

7

INTERVIEWING WITNESSES

COMPONENT FIVE

"

The important thing is not to stop questioning.

- ALBERT EINSTEIN

Upon completing the investigative case review, initial defendant interview, crime scene examination, and background investigation of potential witnesses, witnesses may need to be interviewed. The effective and successful interview of potential witnesses is crucial. Therefore, the criminal defense investigator must be of the highest caliber in this regard. Effective interviewers are not only intelligent but very personable as well. They generally enjoy meeting and talking to different people from all walks of life. Unfortunately, this is a trait which tends to be inbred and not learned, at least not subject to training by the time one has reached adulthood. Therefore, it is advisable to not present an unfriendly or aggressive outward appearance. Such an air could derail an otherwise productive interview. It is also important for the criminal defense investigator to consider the criteria of truth discussed in chapter two. The ability to identify the criteria of truth a witness may have utilized to reach a conclusion can provide significant insight. Empathy can render assistance regarding the perspective of a witness. For example, a witness who was physically abused as a child may observe a simple spanking designed to punish and not injure a child as cruel and severe.

The witnesses should be identified and listed in order of importance. If possible, the witnesses should be contacted via telephone to arrange an appointment to interview them in the criminal defense investigator's office. However, many witnesses often do not have a telephone or are unwilling to travel. Therefore, personal contact at their residence or place of employment may be necessary to secure an interview. In the event an interview cannot be arranged at the office, schedule the interview at a place and time convenient to the witness. In the event an interview is scheduled in a high crime area attempt to arrange the interview in the morning and avoid late afternoon or evening appointments. In criminal cases, witnesses are often difficult to locate. With this in mind, the criminal defense investigator should be prepared to conduct an investigation to locate the witness in order to secure an interview. Sources identified in the background investigation chapter of this text can be of great assistance. Records are often referenced and filed by name. Therefore, review of various records may provide an address or other leads to the location of the witness. In addition, the defendant can also be very helpful in this regard. The defendant may know the witness and be able to provide a home address, place of employment, hang-out, names of relatives or friends, etc.

The criminal defense investigator must also be prepared to conduct an impromptu interview with a witness. Impromptu interviews are frequent and generally occur when the criminal defense investigator is searching for the witness in question. It is very important to be prepared for this encounter. Hard to find witnesses may not appear for a scheduled interview or provide another opportunity to be interviewed in the near future.

Whether the interview is a scheduled interview or an impromptu interview, the criminal defense investigator should be fully prepared for the interview. The preparation of a witness interview is an important factor in the information gathering mission of a witness interview. Interview questions or topics should be prepared in advance to be used as a guide. The interview should be planned in a way that will test the truthfulness of the witness and provide a psychological advantage utilizing superior knowledge of the facts. Remember, the question guide should touch on all of the important questions needed to obtain a complete interview. The question guide should be used only as a guide. Additional questions may arise during the course of the interview and should be pursued. The first question is arguably the only question which can be prepared in advance. The statements and answers provided by the witness will determine the scope and direction of follow-up questions. One can never truly anticipate the statements or answers of a witness. Therefore, it stands to reason that one cannot effectively formulate the next question until one has heard the preceeding answer. Questions should be direct and to the point. However, answers may require more than a "yes" or "no" response. The criminal defense investigator should not be reluctant to pursue each question and answer in great detail. It is important to allow the witness to speak freely and expound on their statements and observations. However, the witness should not be permitted to get off track discussing issues irrelevant to the incident in question. Furthermore, complete control of the interview process should be maintained at all times. Witnesses often move onto other issues during an interview before they have completely covered another issue. It is important to methodically cover every detail of the witness testimony, preferably, in chronological order.

Pursuant to the direction of defense counsel, the criminal defense investigator should attempt to obtain sworn recorded statements of the witnesses. It should be noted that in order to obtain a sworn statement the witness needs to be sworn in by a notary public. A recorded statement is the most accurate record of the interview. However, it is wise to determine the interview and statement method preferred by the attorney representing the defendant.

The following guide may be utilized to assist with sworn recorded statements:

SWORN RECORDED STATEMENT AND INTERVIEW GUIDE

The time is now ___________ am/pm on this _____ day of (month/year). This will be the sworn recorded statement of __________________________________, who resides at ____. This statement is being taken by myself, ______________________, a criminal defense investigator on behalf of the Law Offices of ______________________. This statement is being taken at _____________________________________ in regard to The State of __________________ Vs. __________________. I, _________________________, being a Notary Public will swear in the witness.

Do you, _________________________________, solemnly swear that the statement you are about to provide will be the truth to the best of your knowledge, so help you God? (await answer)

Proceed with the questioning and interview process.

Upon completion, the interview may be terminated in the following manner.

This will terminate this interview of _____________________ on this ____ day of __________ 19 ____, at ___________ am/pm.

Many witnesses do not wish to be recorded and may refuse to be recorded. In the event a witness does not wish to be recorded, it is important to take detailed notes while the interview is in progress. If the witness does not wish the criminal defense investigator to take notes, the criminal defense investigator should comply. It is important to note that witnesses tend to speak more freely when they do not feel threatened. The presence of a recording device or existence of note taking may inhibit the witness and prevent him from being candid. It should also be considered that the recorded statement locks a witness into specific testimony. Dependant upon the ability of the interviewer this may or may not be beneficial. Immediately after the conclusion of the interview a written narrative of the interview should be completed. The narrative should be a complete comprehensive summary of what was said during the interview. The narrative should not be edited and should not exclude any information or statements made by the witness. It is very important not to change the statements or words of a witness. Altering or editing a witness statement can damage the credibility of the witness as well as the criminal defense investigator who obtained the statement.

WITNESS INTERVIEW QUESTIONS

Questions directed at the witness should answer the questions; Who? What? When? Where? How? and Why? The following questions can be used as a general guide when preparing questions prior to conducting a witness interview.

In addition to the full name of the witness, date of birth, social security number, drivers license number, home address, telephone number, and place of employment, variations of the following questions should be directed at the witness.

1. When did the incident they observed occur? Date and time of day?
2. Where? At what location did the incident they observed occur? State, county, city, street, and house number?
3. How many persons were involved? How many others witnessed the incident in question? Identify them or describe?
4. Describe exactly what you observed with your own eyes? (Have the witness go into detail)
5. What was the witness's location in relation to the incident in question? Were there any obstacles obstructing the view of the incident.
6. What were the weather conditions at the time?
7. Does the witness know the defendant? If so, how and for how long?
8. Was the witness interviewed by the police? Did he provide a recorded or written statement? If so, what did he tell the police?
9. Did the witness provide a description of the suspect? If so, what was it?
10. Did the witness assist the police with a composite drawing of the suspect? If so, how accurate does The witness believe the drawing was?
11. At the time of the incident or observation, was the witness tired, frightened, or preoccupied?
12. What is the general health status of the witness?
13. Was the witness ill at the time? Under medication? If so, what type of medication and for what illness?
14. What effect did the medication have on the witness?
15. Had the witness consumed any alcohol or illegal drugs prior to the incident and observations? If so, what?
16. Does the witness wear eyeglasses? Why? Was the witness

wearing the eye glasses at the time of the observations? How far was the witness from the incident observed? (Check the distance)

17. What was the angle of the observations? How long did the witness remain at this angle? Did the witness observe the incident from any other angles?

18. Does the witness have a criminal record? If so, have the witness describe in detail? Jurisdiction, charge, arrest date, disposition, sentence, and time served. (It is wise to ask this question last. This topic can derail an otherwise productive interview)

ALIBI WITNESS INTERVIEW QUESTIONS

1. Were you with the defendant on _________?
2. What time of day were you with the defendant? (do not provide the witness with the time)
3. How do you recall that day?
4. How do you recall that time? Does the witness have a specific reason for remembering the day or time?
5. Where did you first see the defendant on that day?
6. Who else was with the defendant? Identify.
7. Who was with you? Identify.
8. Did anyone else see you and the defendant together? Identify.
9. How long was the defendant with you?
10. How did you know it was the time period you claim?
11. What did the defendant do and say while he was with you? Be as detailed and specific as possible.
12. Did the defendant ever leave your presence during this time period? If so, when? How many times? How long was he gone each time?
13. What was his physical condition when he returned? Was it different from when he left or the same?
14. Was his emotional condition different or the same as when he left?

15. Is the witness related to the defendant?

16. How long has the witness known the defendant?

17. Has the witness ever had any problems with the defendant?
If so, what type? How often? How long ago? Describe problems.

The following are examples of how the proper and effective interview of witnesses can question the credibility of the allegations and contest the prosecution's case.

CASE STUDY: SEXUAL BATTERY

A young African American, promising athlete, and student, found himself the target of sexual battery allegations. A white female reported to police that on December 30, 1993, while listening to music at a friend's house, the defendant "grabbed her by the arm and began pulling her". According to police reports, the defendant forced the alleged victim into a bedroom, pushed her onto a bed, and pulled her pants down. Police reports further reflect that the defendant then forcibly placed his penis inside her vagina. The victim claimed that she was "crying and yelling" for him to stop. According to police reports, the victim did not tell anyone for several days. Subsequently, the victim reported the incident to police resulting in the defendant's arrest.

The defendant's family contacted an attorney who in turn referred them to a private investigator. The private investigator's investigation uncovered several interesting facts. According to defense counsel, "Investigation uncovered evidence to support that the defendant did not commit the offense of Sexual Battery." The report reflected that "several witnesses further support that the parties engaged in sexual intercourse with the mutual consent of both parties".

Based on information obtained from witnesses, testimonial evidence appears to support that the allegations in question were motivated by embarrassment and racial intolerance. The old story of the black suspect, white victim, and white cop? According to witnesses, the victim was forced to report the incident to her parents, telling them that she was forced to have sexual intercourse with a "black male". According to witnesses, the victim could not tell her parents that she had consenting sex with a black male. Interestingly enough, the victim's parents did not report the incident to police. The victim's parents instructed her to have the defendant submit to an AIDS test. Approximately one week later, she contacted the police in an attempt to force the defendant to submit to a test. Subsequently, the defendant was arrested for sexual battery. According to witnesses, prior to her claim of being raped, the victim's family harassed and teased the victim regarding her sexual activity with a black male.

Further information uncovered by the defense investigation revealed that although the victim claimed to have "cried and yelled" for help, two witnesses in the very next room, with only a thin wall to separate them, did not hear her alleged cries. The defense investigation cited several inconsistencies in the alleged victim's statement, including her claim that she was not romantically involved with the defendant. According to witnesses, on the very night in question, she had expressed her intentions and desire to date the defendant.

The defendant was a high school senior, ranked academically in the top 38% of his class. He was a talented member of his high school football team with a promising chance at an athletic scholarship. Teachers, coaches, and parents of friends, provided statements describing the defendant as hard working, honest, reliable, and well mannered.

Testimonial evidence uncovered by the private investigator was turned over to defense counsel.

Subsequently, defense counsel presented the evidence to the prosecution. Based on the witness statements obtained by the private investigator all charges against the defendant were dropped.

CASE STUDY: SEXUAL MISCONDUCT

A Former Florida High School Band Director was the subject of sexual battery allegations by a former female band student. The alleged victim claimed that during the 1989-90 school year the defendant subjected her to various sexual comments and activity. The County School District, the Florida Department of Education, and The State Attorney's Office initiated an investigation into the matter. The State Attorney's Office closed the investigation stating "the band director's conduct with his students is not a criminal matter and will be dealt with by the County School Board. No further action. Case Closed." The State Attorney's Office did not wish to prosecute nor did they wish to commission a thorough criminal investigation. They subsequently referred the matter to the County School Board. Pressure by the County School District and the Florida Department of Education began to weigh upon the defendant. The defendant's concern for his students and lack of financial resources to combat the establishment resulted in the defendant's agreeing to resign his position as Band Director. Under pressure, he also agreed that he would not seek to renew his teaching certificate. The defendant had consulted with an attorney and was under the impression that his resignation would assure a quiet departure without the emotional and mental anguish of media attention.

Unfortunately, news of the allegations, investigation, and resignation were leaked to the press and drew a great deal of media attention, submitting the defendant to nothing less than a character assassination. A year of public humiliation and unemployment followed. However, he slowly began to regain his composure. Rather than run away in shame and disgrace he decided to fight back! He decided that the financial and emotional cost of fighting back was the price of regaining his honor and self esteem. The defendant retained the services of a licensed private investigator and specialist in the area of false allegations of sexual misconduct. A lengthy six month investigation encompassing hundreds of hours of investigation, over fifty detailed witness interviews, and the use of a confidential informant, uncovered documentary and testimonial evidence categorically dismissing the allegations in question. Witnesses were able to provided testimony contesting the allegations one by one. The private investigator's superior knowledge of the facts, combined with his ability to effectively communicate with witnesses on several different levels, resulted in volumes of testimonial evidence supporting the defendant's innocence. The witness interviews were prepared in advance to address specific areas and topics unique to each witness. One by one the allegations were addressed and dismissed with overwhelming testimonial evidence.

However, the major allegation involving sexual intercourse remained unanswered. An interview with the alleged victim would be necessary to negate the allegation. One of the witnesses interviewed during the course of the investigation was a former boyfriend of the alleged victim. He was also a loyal former student and friend of the defendant. The witness was solicited to act as a confidential informant for the private investigator. He agreed and subsequently initiated contact with the alleged victim. The confidential informant was able establish contact with the alleged victim and gain her confidence. Several meetings with the alleged victim revealed a very troubled soul with severe psychological problems. The confidential informant related that she had drastically changed since he dated her several years earlier. The most significant change being her involvement with the occult. Her home was decorated with occult paraphernalia and the walls were painted with murals reflecting satanic symbols. He was debriefed and provided a complete sworn recorded statement following every contact with the alleged victim. As the confidential informant's and the victim's relationship progressed, he became fearful of possible retribution. Fortunately, she had begun to make admissions supporting the defendant's innocence. In fact, the alleged victim related to the confidential informant that she had fabricated the allegations against the defendant. She claimed that she had been pressured by a high school guidance counselor to identify the defendant as the abuser. According to the alleged victim, the incidents in question were purely fantasy. She communicated the incidents with the intention of impressing the guidance counselor. He assured her that the information would remain confidential. Unfortunately, the fantasy took the shape of allegations and snowballed out of control. The nightmare ended when the alleged victim provided a sworn recorded statement to the private investigator recanting the allegations of sexual abuse and characterizing them as false. The defendant's fight to regain his dignity was won through the efforts of an effective criminal defense investigation, specifically, effective witness interviews and professional witness management.

CHAPTER

8

THE REPORT OF INVESTIGATION & TESTIFYING

COMPONENT SIX

"

My parents always told me that people will never know how long it takes you to do something. They will only know how well it is done.

-NANCY HANKS

"

If you tell the truth, you don't have to remember anything.

-MARK TWAIN

Report writing is not only one of the most important elements of a criminal defense investigation but often the most problematic for most criminal defense investigators. Accomplishing the tasks associated with a criminal defense investigation is often done with a much higher degree of success than communicating the results.

The Report of Investigation is a detailed account of a criminal defense investigator's findings associated with the investigation of a case. It is not only important but also crucial that the Report of Investigation is written in a clear, concise, and accurate manner. Communicating the results of an investigation is a vital element to the defense of every case. Therefore, the criminal defense investigator must take the time to ensure that the results of an investigation are written clearly and can be understood by the reader.

The basic categories of criminal defense investigation reflected within this manual may be utilized as a guide to writing an effective report. Investigative results should be reported in chronological order accurately reflecting the actions and information uncovered during the course of investigation. Remember, the report of investigation is the official record of all pertinent information uncovered by the investigation. It is prepared by the criminal defense investigator and submitted to defense counsel. The criminal defense investigator should review, organize, and classify investigative notes and exhibits prior to writing the report. This will assist the criminal defense investigator in writing the report quickly and accurately. The following guidelines should be followed.

1. Arrange your report to present the information uncovered in an orderly manner. Utilize categories and sub-categories to organize the investigative tasks performed and information uncovered.

2. The report should be clear, concise, and grammatically correct.

3. Report all facts uncovered during the course of investigation. The report should reflect everything relevant to prove or disprove the defendant's guilt or innocence.

4. The report must maintain accuracy and attention to detail. The report must maintain impartiality including both favorable and unfavorable details.

5. The report must identify each individual referenced within the report to include; full name, date of birth, social security number, sex, race, address, telephone number, and place of employment.

6. Verify the information uncovered with as many different and independent sources as possible.

7. The report must be complete answering the following questions: Who? What? Where? When? How? and Why?

8. The report should be brief and to the point. However, do not sacrifice completeness and accuracy in order to achieve brevity.

Completing the investigation and forwarding the written report of investigation to defense counsel may or may not be the final task of the criminal defense investigator. As in most types of investigation, the criminal defense investigator will often be called to testify. The effective testimony of the criminal defense investigator may be crucial in assisting the court to reach a decision as to the defendant's guilt or innocence. Therefore, proper preparation is a basic factor in determining the effectiveness of the criminal defense investigator's testimony. When appearing as a witness it is important to maintain a true and sincere sense of objectivity and impartiality at all times.

The following procedures may be used to prepare for testimony:

1. Review original notes, diagrams, and photographs.
2. Review reports of investigation.
3. Prepare and assemble all notes, diagrams, photographs, and reports in an organized manner for easy and quick reference.
4. Check your appearance prior to testifying. Maintain a professional appearance at all times.

Effective testimony requires skill, tact, and self-confidence. Events must be described accurately leaving the conclusions of guilt or innocence to the court. Maintain a good and positive attitude. Use a confident, professional, and conversational tone. Speak loudly and clearly directing answers to the jury. Listen to every question before answering and be sure each question is understood before attempting to answer. In addition, confine answers to the question. Do not volunteer additional information unless it is specifically requested. Never testify to information that was not obtained through personal knowledge. Do not hesitate to correct a mistake or misspoken statement. A witness will often be asked to answer categorically such as yes or no. However, a yes or no answer may not be complete or may be misleading. In such a case, immediately ask to further explain the answer. It is also proper to request permission to refer to notes, diagrams, photographs, or reports. Remember, testimony must be limited to factual information personally observed, felt, heard, smelled, tasted, stated, or accomplished by the criminal defense investigator. Only if asked, should the criminal defense investigator depart from this to render an opinion or conclusion. Never, under any circumstances, argue with the attorney conducting the examination or cross-examination. Attorneys will often attempt to bait a witness into arguing or losing ones temper in order to taint the credibility of the witness.

EXAMPLE SCENARIO: ARREST AFFIDAVIT & REPORT OF INVESTIGATION

The following report of investigation is provided as an example and reference. The report is based upon the example scenario arrest affidavit. The scenario is utilized by the 19th Judicial Circuit Office of the Public Defender as part of the Public Defender Investigator Training Program operating under the direction of the author. The report of investigation was submitted by Rich Grego, an honors graduate and instructor with the program. The exhibits and attachments identified as B thru E within the scenario report of investigation are not enclosed for reference.

Review of the arrest affidavit will allow the reader to understand how the writer utilized the component method of criminal defense investigation. The report is also an example of how to effectively communicate the results of his investigation.

ARREST AFFIDAVIT

DEFENDANT: Doe, John W. a/k/a "Bo-Bo"
ADDRESS: 215 Binney Drive, Fort Pierce, Florida
TELEPHONE: No telephone

SEX: Male HEIGHT: 5'7" WEIGHT: 150 RACE: Black
EYE COLOR: Brown HAIR COLOR: Black DATE OF BIRTH: 3/06/68
CLOTHING: Black Chicago Bulls cap, red shirt, blue jeans, white tennis shoes

SOCIAL SECURITY NUMBER: 212-031-0450
OCCUPATION: Unemployed
DISTINGUISHING MARKS: None visible

ARREST DATE: 10/30/94 TIME: 9:45 p.m. ADDRESS: Seaway Drive/S. Bridge

OFFENSE DATE: 10/30/94 TIME: 7:30 p.m. ADDRESS: 111 Atlantic Ave.

INVESTIGATING OFFICER: J.E. Hoover, Fort Pierce Police Department

CHARGE: Burglary of a Structure

SUMMARY OF OFFENSES AND PROBABLE CAUSE FOR AFFIDAVIT: On October 30, 1994, 7:35 p.m., officers from the Fort Pierce Police Department responded to ABC Insurance, 111 Atlantic Avenue, Fort Pierce, Florida in reference to a report of burglary. Upon arrival, officers found the side door/entry ajar. Signs of forced entry were present on the door jam and locking mechanism. Attempts to lift latent prints from the door and entry point met with negative results.

Contact with the complainant, Ann Smith, revealed that one IBM 486X computer, one color monitor, and one laser printer were missing from the office. An inventory by Ann Smith revealed that no additional items were missing. Ann Smith related that she was the last one to leave the building at approximately 6:30 p.m. Smith related that she exited via the side/west door, securing the door as she departed. Smith walked across the street to the parking lot behind the Sun Bank to her car. Ann Smith related that she observed two individuals in the area. A maintenance man was working in the parking lot adjacent to the St. Lucie County Public Library on Indian River Drive. Smith recalls the white male, wearing khaki pants and shirt, and cutting the grass. Smith also observed a young black male, wearing a red shirt, and standing on the corner of 2nd Street and Atlantic Avenue. No suspect at this time.

At 7:55 p.m., Detective Sherlock established contact with Al Dente, a maintenance man with the St. Lucie County Public Library. Al Dente related that he was working in front of the library, cutting the hedges with a weedeater. At approximately 6:50 p.m., Mr. Dente heard a loud bang. According to Mr. Dente, it sounded like a hammer hitting something. Approximately 10 minutes later, Mr. Dente observed a black male carrying a large object depart from the side door of the ABC Insurance Agency and run west on Atlantic Avenue. Approximately 2-3 minutes later, Mr. Dente observed the same black male, wearing a red shirt and blue jeans, turn east around the corner on 2nd Street and Orange Avenue and walk through the public parking lot north on Indian River Drive. Al Dente provided a description of the subject as a young black male, approximately 6 feet, 200 pounds, wearing a red shirt and blue jeans. Al Dente's description was provided to dispatch for distribution to patrol units in the area.

Unit #17, Officer I.M. Tough, contacted Detective Sherlock and related that he had a young black male matching the description of the suspect in custody. The suspect was observed walking east over the South Bridge toward South Beach. Subsequently, the suspect was transported to the scene where he was positively identified by the witness as the suspect in question. The suspect, identified as John Doe, denied the allegation but admitted to being in the area of Atlantic Avenue and 2nd Street at approximately 6:30 - 7:00 p.m. The suspect was read Miranda Warnings and requested an attorney. The suspect was arrested and transported to the St. Lucie County Jail.

REPORT OF INVESTIGATION

DATE OF REPORT: 04/10/97

FILE REFERENCE: State of Florida v. John Doe
St. Lucie County, Florida
Docket Number 94-001-CF

AGENCY FILE NO: 94-001-CF

REQUESTED BY: Brandon A. Perron, Program Director
Office of the Public Defender

INVESTIGATOR: Rich Grego, P.D.I.
Public Defender Investigator

SECTION I

INFORMATION: Pursuant to the request of Defense Counsel an investigation was conducted regarding the referenced matter. Refer to Arrest Affidavit (Exhibit A) for further information and details.

SECTION II

SYNOPSIS: The following investigation was conducted pursuant to accepted investigative procedure and guidelines. Investigative efforts included but were not limited to Investigative Review & Analysis, Defendant Interview, Crime Scene Examination & Inspection, Background Investigation/Records Research, Witness Interviews, and the construction of a time line of events relevant to the facts presented and uncovered during the course of investigation.

The following witnesses were identified by the defense and interviewed;

A) Albert Sims, white male, born 03/16/54,
social security number 037-51-3997,
334 28th Street, Port St. Lucie, Florida, 34958

B) Jack Miranda, white male, 6', 180",
Born 11/28/67, social security number 265-43-5669
10 South 13 Street, Fort Pierce, Florida 34951

SECTION III

INVESTIGATIVE CASE REVIEW: On 02/10/97, Public Defender Investigator Rich Grego conducted a case review and analysis of the Arrest Affidavit (Exhibit A). During the course of investigation a number of inconsistencies were discovered between the testimony given in the foregoing documents and interviews as well as inconsistencies internal to the documents and interviews themselves. The following inconsistencies were noted:

1) The defendant's (John Doe) social security number appears to be incorrectly recorded as a result of the existence of an extra digit.

2) The referenced "Investigating Officer", identified as J.E. Hoover, Fort Pierce Police Department, is not mentioned in regard to investigating the incident in any part of the narrative.

3) The narrative related that the responding officers, having been given a description of an individual matching that of the defendant, did not regard this individual as a suspect at the time of their initial investigation (approximately 07:35 p.m.)

4) The narrative relates that the description of a possible suspect given to an investigating officer identified as Det. Sherlock at 07:55 p.m. by a witness identified as Al Dente was that of a black male approximately 6' tall and weighing 200 lbs. However, the narrative goes on to relate that the defendant, who is described as being 5'7" tall and weighing 150 lbs., was taken into custody by Officer Tough, who claimed to have a suspect "matching the description".

5) The narrative relates that the defendant claimed to have been in the area of the incident between 06:30 - 07:00 p.m. However, the "Offense Time" listed above (in the affidavit) is 07:30 p.m.

SECTION IV

DEFENDANT INTERVIEW: On 02/20/97, P.D.I. Rich Grego proceeded to St. Lucie Co. Jail to interview the defendant, John Doe. (Hereinafter referred to as defendant).

The Defendant related that he lives at 215 Binney Drive in a white and blue house approximately 1/4 mile off Seaway Drive in Fort Pierce, Florida. He has resided there with his mother (his father, Henry Doe, is deceased) since he was ten years old. He is currently 29 years old. He smokes marijuana occasionally and is a social drinker. His prior criminal record consists of a 1992 DUI arrest that resulted in a

Reckless Driving adjudication for which he received two years probation and a year suspended license. He has not reapplied for a license and does not drive.

Defendant relates that on 10/28/94 or 10/29/94, he made an appointment by telephone with an unidentified female for a job interview at Sterling's Clothing Store on the corner of 2nd Street and Orange Avenue, Fort Pierce. The appointment was set for 10/30/94 at 06:30 p.m., at which time Defendant was to meet Mr. Sims, identified as the manager of the store.

He further related that a couple of days prior to the interview he met with a friend (known only as "cheeseburger") who was fishing beneath the South Bridge and agreed to meet him at the River Raw Bar following the interview. The River Raw Bar is located at the foot of the South Bridge approximately one mile from Sterling's or 20-30 minutes walking time. He related that he and Cheeseburger often drink and hang-out at the River Raw Bar.

On 10/30/94 the defendant remained at home until 05:45 p.m. and did not communicate with anyone during this time. At approximately 05:45 p.m. the defendant departed on foot for the interview walking east on Binney Drive to Seaway Drive over the South Bridge to Indian River Drive south to Orange Avenue (which he accessed by cutting across the parking lot across the street from the library) to Sterling's at the corner of 2nd Street. While passing the library, the defendant observed a white male maintenance man, wearing a Khaki color uniform, cutting the grass or shrubs in front of the library.

The Defendant arrived at Sterling's at approximately 06:20 p.m. He attempted to open the door and, finding it locked, looked inside. Seeing, no one, he then proceeded across the street to the north east corner of Atlantic Avenue and 2nd Street, where he stood and smoked a cigarette. He remained there until approximately 06:35 p.m. when Mr. Sims arrived for the appointment. While standing at 2nd and Atlantic between (approximately) 06:20 and 06:35, the defendant heard a loud metallic sounding bang followed by a quieter bang and a clicking sound. He observed a black male (6', 200 lbs.) emerge from a building on the south side of Atlantic and cross the street north to the parking lot on the east side of Sun Trust Bank. The black male was wearing a business suit, carrying a briefcase, and speaking on a cellular phone. At this point the defendant lost sight of the black male. Several minutes later a white female emerged from a parking area on the south side of Atlantic and also walked north into Sun Trust Bank parking lot, where she disappeared from sight. The Defendant was unable to provide a further description of the white female.

At approximately 06:35 p.m. (or fifteen minutes after defendant's arrival at Sterling's) Mr. Sims arrived in front of Sterling's in a silver/grey Mercedes (four door) where he met the defendant. Mr. Sims is described as a white male in his forties with grey hair. According to the Defendant, Mr. Sims apologized for being late and the two then entered the store together. The interview lasted approximately 30 minutes and took place in the 2nd floor office of Sterling's. The Defendant claims that he did not see or hear anyone or anything else during this time. According to the defendant, the interview went well and he believes that he got the job. The defendant stated that the interview ended prior to 07:15 p.m. and bases his statement on his claim that Mr. Sims needed to make a phone call at this time. Mr. Sims walked defendant to the door and locked it behind him.

The Defendant then proceeded east on Orange Avenue. Just outside of Sterling's, The defendant recalls seeing an unidentified individual smoking a cigarette and standing on the east side of 2nd Street approximately 100 ft. south of his position. Though darkness did not permit the defendant to see the individual, he estimated his location by the glow of the lit cigarette.

The Defendant crossed the parking lot across from the library to access Indian River Drive going north. During this time defendant observed a white maintenance man wearing Khaki pants, ear muffs, eye goggles, and using a weed blower in front of the library. According to the Defendant, the maintenance man was giving him dirty looks resulting in the defendant making an obscene gesture in the way of extending his middle finger to the maintenance man. The Defendant proceeded further and observed a white maintenance van parked on Indian River Drive just north of the library.

Proceeding north on Indian River Drive, the defendant arrived at the River Raw Bar approximately 15 or 20 minutes after leaving Sterling's (7:20-7:30 p.m.). He was joined by Cheeseburger approximately 10 minutes later. Cheeseburger's real name is unknown but the defendant believes it might be "Jack". He is a white male with blond hair approximately 6' tall. He may work at The Orange-Way Packing House next door to the Raw Bar. The defendant knows Cheeseburger primarily through socializing at this bar which Cheeseburger frequents after work. On the evening of the incident, the Defendant and Cheeseburger drank 2-3 draft beers and ate chicken wings and nachos (that Cheeseburger paid for). The Defendant only recalls speaking to "Steve the Bartender" beside Cheeseburger on this occasion. Steve is a white male and spoke to the two on and off while they were there.

The Defendant and Cheeseburger departed the bar at approximately 9:30 p.m. Cheeseburger walked south down Indian River Drive while the

Defendant proceeded east over South Bridge (Seaway Drive). While walking across the bridge the Defendant was passed by a police car that stopped in front him. When he walked past the car, a police officer exited the vehicle, apprehended him, and took him into custody. While in the police car the officer asked him if he had been in the vicinity of Atlantic and Orange Avenues that evening. He replied "Yes", but did not elaborate. The Defendant was driven to the Fort Pierce Library where he was identified as having committed a "break-in" by the maintenance man with whom he had the altercation. He was then transported to St. Lucie Co. Jail and read Miranda Warning. He was given a $5,000 bond and has not spoken with anyone since his arrest.

SECTION V

CRIME SCENE: On 03/20/97 at 1:30 p.m. P.D.I. Rich Grego accomplished an examination of the crime scene area in question.

DESCRIPTION: The crime scene area is described as a heavily trafficked grid of streets in the downtown business district of the city of Fort Pierce, Florida. It is well-lit during the evening hours by a number of street lights, lamp-post lights, and interior/exterior store-front lights. Long distance vision and observations in this area, however, would appear to be obstructed considerably by parked cars/trucks, trees, mailboxes, and buildings.

A diagram of the vicinity includes the streets and structures relevant to the incident as well as distances relevant to the allegations. (Refer to Exhibit B). Photographs of the crime scene were accomplished and are depicted in a photograph diagram. (Refer to Exhibit C). Photographs are cataloged by number and reflected within a photograph log. (Refer to Exhibit D)

REFER TO EXHIBITS B, C, AND D, RESPECTIVELY FOR ADDITIONAL DETAILS.

SECTION VI

BACKGROUND INVESTIGATION: Pursuant to the request of defense counsel a comprehensive background investigation was conducted regarding the listed witnesses. Examination of Statewide Criminal History Records, County Criminal Records, Civil Court Records, and Motor Vehicle Records met with negative results.

SECTION VII

WITNESS INTERVIEWS:

A) Albert Sims, white male, born 03/16/54,
social security number 037-51-3997,
334 28th Street, Port St. Lucie, Florida, 34958

On 4/09/97 at 1:30 p.m. P.D.I. Rich Grego conducted an interview of a potential defense witness identified as Mr. Albert Sims. The interview was not recorded and was conducted at the Office of the Public Defender. Albert Sims is described as a white male, born 03/16/54, social security number 037-51-3997, residing at 334 28th Street, Port St. Lucie, Florida, 34958.

Mr. Sims confirmed John Doe's (hereinafter referred to as "defendant") statement that an interview was arranged over the phone by Sims secretary with the defendant for 10/30/94. The call was made several days prior to 10/30, in response to an advertisement for the position of store clerk in the Fort Pierce Tribune. Sims stated further that a Sunday evening interview was normal procedure for him. The interview was scheduled for 6:30 p.m. at Sterling's Clothing Store which he owns and manages.

Sims stated that on 10/30/94 he met the defendant in front of Sterling's at 6:35/6:40 p.m. Sims arrived for the interview in his 1995 silver/grey mercedes, 4 door. He travelled directly from his home driving north on US #1 to Orange Avenue and east to Sterling's. When he arrived the defendant was standing alone on the north east corner of 2nd and Atlantic Avenue. Upon meeting the defendant Sim's greeted him and apologized for being late. They then went into the store and proceeded to a second floor office for an interview. Sims noted that when he arrived at Roslows, the lighting outside was minimal describing it as "dusk".

Sims stated that the interview with the defendant went well. He related that he would have given the defendant the job if he had not been arrested. Sims added that the defendant did not act nervous, confused, upset, or in any way unusual in Sims' estimation. Sims ended the interview just prior to 7:15 p.m. stating he makes a regularly scheduled telephone call to a supplier at this time.

At the end of the interview, Sims walked the defendant to the door of Sterling's and locked it behind him. He observed the defendant depart on foot and travel east down Orange Avenue. He remembers nothing unusual on the street at this time and observed no one else in the area. He added that it was very dark outside at the time of the defendant's departure.

Sims related that he made his telephone call and completed paperwork in from approximately 7:15 p.m. to approximately 10:00 p.m. At 10:00 p.m. he exited Sterling's. At this time he observed a silhouetted figure south of his position on 2nd Street approximately 100 feet standing on the east side of the road. Sims entered his vehicle and drove south on 2nd Street and noted a van with two silhouetted figures (one outside, one inside) parked on the east side of Depot Drive. The figure outside the van was "dark complexioned" but of unknown race/gender. Darkness prevented his obtaining a better description.

B) Jack Miranda, white male, 6', 180",
Born 11/28/67, social security number 265-43-5669
10 South 13th Street, Fort Pierce, Florida 34951

On 4/10/97 at 1:30 p.m. P.D.I. Rich Grego proceeded to the Orange-Way Packing House to interview the individual identified as "Cheeseburger" or "Jack" by John Doe (hereinafter referred to as "defendant"). Upon arriving at Orange-Way's, the manager identified as Joseph Cheatham was contacted and questioned regarding the identify of "Cheeseburger." Cheatham identified the subject in question as Jack Miranda and had him paged to the front office where a private interview was conducted. The interview was not recorded.

Jack Miranda is described as a white male, 6', 180", employed as a maintenance man for Orange-Way. He states that he remembers the evening in question. Miranda further recalls making a date to meet the defendant whom he describes as a friend, known to him as "Bo", several days prior to 10/30/94 when he and the defendant were conversing at the foot of the South Bridge in Fort Pierce. According to Miranda, he and the defendant agreed to meet at the River Raw Bar following the defendant's interview.

Miranda stated that on 10/30/94 he departed his residence on foot at about 6:30 p.m. with the River Raw Bar as his destination. He recalls the approximate times of events in question because he was wearing a watch. Miranda did not recall the precise route he took to reach the bar. In fact he gave two versions of his trip to the bar during the interview, one being that he walked the entire distance but does not remember his route. In the second version he described meeting friends at a convenience store on US Highway #1 and driving around with them until approximately 7:30 p.m., when they dropped him off at the bar. Miranda refused to identify the identity of his friends or explain the conflicting statements.

Miranda stated that he met the defendant at the bar and that the defendant was already inside the bar when he arrived. He did not remember what the defendant was wearing but said that the defendant "always" wears a black and red in color Chicago Bulls baseball style cap. He recalled the defendant saying something about having a fight "or something" that evening and recalls having 5 or 6 beers with the defendant, which Miranda purchased. Although he did not remain in visual contact with the defendant during the entire time that they were at the bar, Miranda does not believe that the defendant left the bar at any time.

Miranda and the defendant exited the bar at approximately 9:30 p.m. He observed the defendant walk east over the South Bridge as he walked home. Once again, Miranda claimed that he does not recall his route.

Miranda stated he "heard" of the defendant's arrest the following day but would not elaborate. He did not recall from whom he received this information. (No Further Information)

SECTION VIII

911 RECORD: Based upon information noted within the Arrest Affidavit the 911 records referencing the incident in question were obtained from the Department of Public Safety. (Refer to Exhibit E)

1) Review of the 911 document indicated that on 10/30/94 at 19:08 hours or 7:08 p.m., 911 received a call indicating the presence of suspicious activity/persons carrying "unknown items" at 111 Atlantic Avenue. The document indicated further that three police units were dispatched in response to the report. Identification of the responding officers is reflected by identification number only. The records reflects that Officer #17 arrived at 7:18 p.m. and departed at 7:21 pm. Officer #21 arrived at 7:22 pm and departed at 7:55 pm, and #11 which arrived at 7:55 pm and departed at 9:55 pm.

A) The first officer on the scene would have been officer Tough (Unit 17) who later arrested the defendant--and who interviewed Ann Smith.

B) The third responding unit (Unit #11) would have been Det. Sherlock who interviewed Al Dente.

C) The affidavit reflects that incident time as 7:30 p.m. However, the initial 911 call is recorded at 7:08 p.m.

D) Officer Tough (Unit #17) had arrived on the scene, investigated the incident, and departed by 7:22 p.m.--nine minutes before the incident in the arrest affidavit is listed as occurring.

E) According to Al Dente's testimony as reflected within the Arrest Affidavit, he witnessed the incident between 6:50 and 7:05 p.m. The perpetrator had departed the area by 7:08 p.m., which is when the 911 document indicates that suspicious persons were in the area.

F) The 911 document indicates that two suspicious individuals were involved while the affidavit indicates (via Al Dente's testimony) that only one individual was involved. (Refer to Exhibit E/911 Records for further information)

SECTION IX

TIMELINE OF EVENTS: Based upon information documented with the arrest affidavit and evidence uncovered during the course of the foregoing investigation, a timeline of events was constructed.

5:40 p.m. - Sunset, no moon/overcast. (Source: Fort Pierce Tribune)

5:45 p.m.- Defendant leaves home on foot for interview. (Defendant)

5:45 p.m.- 6:20 p.m. - Defendant west over S. Bridge, Indian River Dr., Orange Avenue to 2nd Street. (Defendant)

5:45 p.m. - 6:20 p.m. - Defendant observes Khaki maintenance man at library. (Defendant)

6:20 p.m. - Defendant arrives at Sterling's, door locked. (Defendant)

6:20 p.m. - 6:30 p.m. - Defendant hears a metallic "bang" (Defendant)

6:20 p.m. - 6:30 p.m. - Defendant sees black male on Atlantic Avenue. (Defendant)

6:20 p.m. - 6:30 p.m. - Defendant sees unidentified white woman. (Defendant)

6:20 p.m. - 6:30 p.m. - Defendant smokes on the corner of 2nd Street and Atlantic Avenue. (Defendant)

6:30 p.m. - J. Miranda leaves residence for Raw Bar. (Jack Miranda)

6:30 p.m. - Ann Smith exits ABC Insurance building. (Arrest Affidavit)

6:35 p.m. - 6:40 p.m. - Interview with Mr. Sims begins. (Defendant & A. Sims)

6:50 p.m. - Al Dente hears a loud bang. (Arrest Affidavit)

6:50 p.m. - Al Dente observes 6', 200 lbs. black male exit side door and run west on Atlantic. (Arrest Affidavit)

7:05 p.m. - Al Dente observes same black male east on the corner of Atlantic Avenue and Orange - parking lot north on Indian River Drive. (Arrest Affidavit)

7:08 p.m. - 911 call received reporting suspicious persons at 111 Atlantic Avenue. (911 Records)

7:10 p.m. - 7:15 p.m. - Defendant exits interview. (Defendant & A. Sims)

7:10 p.m. - 7:15 p.m. - Defendant sees unidentified individual. (Defendant)

7:15 p.m. - 7:20 p.m. - Defendant has altercation with white male in Khaki uniform. (Defendant)

7:18 p.m. - Unit #17 arrives at incident scene (911 Records)

7:20 p.m. - 7:30 p.m. - Defendant proceeds to the Raw Bar (Defendant)

7:30 p.m. - Defendant meets Miranda at Raw Bar. (Defendant & Jack Miranda)

7:30 p.m. - Offense committed (Arrest Affidavit)

7:35 p.m. - Officers respond (Arrest Affidavit)

7:35 p.m. - 1st report filed, no suspect (Arrest Affidavit)

7:55 p.m. - Det. Sherlock contacts Al Dente. (Arrest Affidavit)

9:30 p.m. - Defendant leaves River Raw Bar east on South Bridge. (Defendant)

9:30 p.m. - Miranda leaves the River Raw Bar. (Jack Miranda)

9:45 p.m. - Defendant is arrested. (Arrest Affidavit)

10:00 p.m. - Sims leaves Sterling's, observes suspicious subjects/van. (A. Sims)

SECTION X

SUMMARY OF INVESTIGATION: Based upon information uncovered during the course of the investigation, the following observations, analysis, and recommendations were generated to assist defense counsel:

1) The defendant's interview indicates that he arrived at the area of the incident at approximately 6:20 p.m. and entered Roslows for his interview at approximately 6:35-6:40 p.m. His presence on the north east corner of Atlantic Avenue and 2nd Street is partially confirmed by Ann Smith (Arrest Affidavit, Exhibit A) who witnessed an individual matching the defendant's description at this location at 6:30 p.m. His presence at the same location at 6:35-6:40 p.m. is confirmed by Albert Sims (witness interview A).

2) The above would indicate that any involvement by the defendant in the incident would have to have taken place between approximately 6:30 and 6:40 p.m., (since the police were investigating the offense by 7:18, according to 911 records, the defendant could not in all likelihood have commited the offense after his interview, which ended at approximately 7:15 p.m.

3) The Arrest Affidavit (via Al Dente's testimony) indicates that the offense very likely took place between approximately 6:50-7:05 p.m.-- which would be inconsistent with the allegation that the offense was committed by the defendant, who would have been in an interview at Roslows at this time.

4) Several inconsistencies regarding defendants' description exist within the Arrest Affidavit (discussed in sect. 3, Case Review).

5) Al Dente's assertion (Arrest Affidavit) that he observed the defendant exiting the side door of ABC Insurance and run west on Atlantic Avenue carrying a large object is dubious. His stated location in front of the library makes a view of ABC's side door impossible, and even viewing the front door of ABC from this vantage point involves 460 feet of terrain obstructed by palm trees, signs and often, parked cars. (Refer Exhibits B and C). Further, from Dente's apparent location there is almost no visibility of Atlantic Avenue west of ABC Insurance. Dente's assertion that he observed the defendant turn the corner of Orange and 2nd Street and proceed north on Indian River Drive is also improbable from Dente's stated location, as his vision of the corner of Orange Avenue and 2nd Street remains obstructed by the bank office building on the south side and the office building on the north side of Orange Avenue. (Refer to Exhibits B and C).

6) Albert Sims' testimony (sect 7, A) largely corroborates the defendant's statement in terms of times and locations during the evening of 10/30/94. He also noted that at least two other suspects were in the area that evening. Albert Sim's claims that this information was conveyed to Det. Sherlock of the Fort Pierce Police Department.

7) Jack Miranda corroborates the defendant's statement regarding the

time-frame that he was at the River Raw Bar on 10/30/94. Miranda might be described as an uncooperative witness. His testimony regarding his movements during the time of the incident is contradictory. He was with at least two other people in an unidentified truck between 6:30 and 7:30 p.m., according to his own testimony. (Sect.7,B).

8) The 911 records investigation revealed several inconsistencies between the incident-times and number of persons as recorded in the arrest affidavit. (Further details elaborated in sect. 8).

9) A. The foregoing information reveals that the defendant had a very narrow time frame in which to commit the offense (5 to 10 minutes.)

B. The foregoing information reveals that the defendant was identified as the perpetrator by Al Dente:
1) from a long and obstructed distance in dim lighting.
2) as substantially different in height and weight then he actually is.
3) after having a verbal altercation with Dente.
4) as having committed the offense during a time frame (6:50-7:05 p.m.) when he could not have been where he was alleged to have been.

C. The forgoing information reveals that the Arrest Affidavit differs substantially with the 911 documents regarding times and number of perpetrators.

D. The forgoing information reveals that the Arrest Affidavit contradicts itself in several respects.

E. The forgoing information reveals that a number possible alternative suspects have yet to be identified.

10) It is recommended that the defendant's involvement on this incident be considered questionable and that the possibility of alternative suspects be explored.

SECTION XI

EXHIBITS AND ATTACHMENTS: The following exhibits and attachments accompany this report and are referenced within the report.

Exhibit A - Arrest Affidavit.
Exhibit B - Crime Scene Area Diagram.
Exhibit C - Crime Scene Area Photograph Diagram
Exhibit D - Photograph Log and Photographs 1-24.
Exhibit E - Department of Public Safety 911 Records.

STATUS: Case Closed pending further requests.

PREPARED BY:

Rich Greco
RICH GREGO
PUBLIC DEFENDER INVESTIGATOR

REVIEWED & APPROVED BY;

Brandon A. Perron
BRANDON A. PERRON
TRAINING PROGRAM DIRECTOR

An accurate, concise, and effectively written report of investigation will provide closure for the investigation. The written report will document findings and demonstrate the methodical approach and course of the investigation. An effective written report will allow the reader to follow the criminal defense investigator's logical and effective utilization of the component method.

CHAPTER

9

THE INVESTIGATION OF DOMESTIC VIOLENCE CRIMES

"

When two people are under the
influence of the most violent,
most insane, most delusive,
most transient of passions,
they are required to swear
that they will remain in that
excited, abnormal,
and exhausting condition
continuously until death do
them part.

-GEORGE BERNARD SHAW

The O.J. Simpson case successfully glued millions of Americans to their television sets awaiting the latest developments in one of the most famous murder cases in American history. The tragic murders of Nicole Brown Simpson and Ronald Goldman and the subsequent acquittal of O.J. Simpson set the stage for an in-depth look at our criminal justice system and a national analysis into the issue of domestic violence. It's truly unfortunate that it would take such a horrible crime to spark serious debate about a problem that has arguably reached epidemic proportions. According to the F.B.I., over 4 million American women are physically abused each year, often resulting in murder. Some sources report that a domestic assault occurs in one of every six American households every 15 seconds. According to the American Academy of Family Physicians, victims of domestic violence range from age 16 to 66. Fifty one-percent of the victims are current or former girlfriends of the batterer and 47 percent are wives. The U.S. Department of Health and Human Services reports that one-fifth to one-third of all women are physically abused during their lifetime and half of the murdered women in the United States are killed by a current or former partner. In addition, violence by women is often in retaliation or self defense. Women commit only 8 percent of all homicides in the United States, but 51 percent of them are against partners with a history of spouse abuse.

The criminal defense investigator is in a unique position. Defense counsel may often request that the criminal defense investigator to conduct an investigation on behalf of a batterer. However, the lines are not always drawn clearly. Based on statistics, it would appear that 51 percent of the women who commit a homicide are victims forced to retaliate or defend themselves against a batterer. Unfortunately, the victim who is forced to defend herself may be subject to criminal prosecution. The criminal defense investigator may find himself in the unique position of having a victim-batterer and a victim-defendant. Therefore, it is highly probable that a criminal defense investigator may be called upon to uncover evidence to support a theory of defense based on the Battered Woman Syndrome. The Battered Woman Syndrome is a sub-category of the most common psychological diagnosis observed in battered woman identified as Post Traumatic Stress Disorder (PTSD). PTSD is based on the concept that a person who is exposed to danger or trauma is expected to have specific psychological responses. The responses are divided into several categories including memory changes and the "Fight or Flight" response. The "Fight or Flight" response is often encountered in a criminal defense investigation where the defendant was forced to fight with no option of flight.

In addition to assisting defense counsel, the criminal defense investigator's function may be to support the forensic psychologist. The forensic psychologist may be tasked with conducting an assessment to determine if the defendant suffers from Battered Woman Syndrome. Several sources of information will be required by the forensic psychologist in order to form a credible opinion. The criminal defense investigator's task is to uncover independent evidence to support a history of domestic violence. Unfortunately, in many cases eye witnesses of domestic violence are not available. The absence of significant testimonial evidence may require the investigation to focus on uncovering documentary evidence to corroborate a history of domestic violence.

The following sources may assist the criminal defense investigator's search for documentary evidence:

1) Police Reports
2 911 Records/Recordings
3) Court Records
4) Rape Crisis Lines
5) Battered Women Shelters
6) Emergency Room/Hospital Records
7) Therapist Records

Because of the complexity of domestic violence crimes it is very important for criminal defense investigators to ensure that they are properly trained. The following guidelines should be followed and incorporated into reports when investigating crimes involving domestic violence.

GUIDELINES FOR INVESTIGATING DOMESTIC VIOLENCE CRIMES

1. OBTAIN A DETAILED STATEMENT FROM THE VICTIM.
   Use the victim's exact words whenever possible.

Questions to ask a suspected victim of domestic violence in an initial interview;

a) Have you ever been punched, bitten, hit, pushed, or otherwise hurt by your partner?

b) Do you feel emotionally abused by your partner?

c) Has your partner ever forced you to have sex?

d) Are you afraid of your partner?

e) Do you believe your partner tries to control you?

Note: In the event a victim shares information that she is battered it is important to listen. Inform the victim that they are not to blame for the abuse - it's not her fault her partner abuses her - she does not deserve to be treated this way. Explain the choices available for the victim to escape the abuse. Remember, the victim must be allowed to make her own choices. You cannot make the decision for the victim.

Obtain a complete statement from the victim. Do not be judgmental. Document all information provided by the victim. Reflect the victim's statements in quotes. Do not paraphrase.

If the victim identifies the abuser, again quote the victim.

2. **NOTE THE VICTIM'S EMOTIONAL STATE.**
Be specific about the victim's emotional state (e.g., crying, shouting, fearful)

3. **DESCRIBE AND DOCUMENT INJURIES.**
Describe observable injuries in detail, (e.g., "...a two inch cut over the right eye.") Ask the victim whether she/he sustained other injuries that may not be visible and document them in writing, i.e. pain, soreness. Photograph the victim's injuries prior to medical treatment.

Victims of domestic violence may sometimes delay reporting an incident. Such delays may result in the lack of physical evidence to support a history of domestic violence. However, a progressive photographic technique, Reflective Ultraviolet Photography, can document injuries on flesh as old as nine months after they have healed. The technique identifies pattern injuries which have a recognizable pattern or shape. Pattern injuries include but are not limited to: bruising, contusions, abrasions, scratches, bite marks, belt marks, and cigarette burns. A forensic photographer should be consulted in order to determine if evidence of pattern injury can be recovered utilizing the Reflective Ultraviolet Photography technique.

4. **OBTAIN INFORMATION ABOUT PAST ABUSE.**
History of abuse or violence is used by the legal counsel in determining the best course of legal action. Documented past abuse can be used as evidence. This information is also helpful to other agencies in determining an appropriate level of intervention.

5. **OBTAIN A DETAILED STATEMENT FROM THE BATTERER.**
Whenever possible use his/her exact words. Document his/her emotional state and any threatening comments the batterer makes to the victim or witnesses.

6. **DESCRIBE THE SCENE.**
The report should describe any evidence of an altercation, i.e., broken items, furniture tipped over, etc. Photograph and diagram the scene.

7. **INTERVIEW OTHER WITNESSES.**
In addition to taking statements, record the full name, address and telephone number of each witness.

8. **NOTE OTHER INFORMATION.**
Record information necessary to charge other offenses such as criminal damage to property, trespassing, terroristic threats, etc.

9. **REFLECT THE DECISION AND CONCLUSIONS OF THE RESPONDING POLICE OFFICERS.**
An arrest report should indicate how the officer concluded that he/she had probable cause to make an arrest. If an arrest was not made, a detailed report should still be filed. It is particularly important to document the officer's conclusions about any injuries. Injury is not in itself sufficient evidence to establish probable cause that an assault has occurred. The officer must conclude from all of the evidence that the injury was intentionally inflicted in an act other than self defense.

10. **NOTE MULTIPLE ARRESTS.**
If an officer makes a multiple arrest, the report should separately document how probable cause was established for each individual arrested.

COLLECTION OF EVIDENCE

The investigator should preserve evidence that may be used in court to support the allegation of domestic violence. Typically, evidence such as photographs of the scene, diagrams of the scene, and photographs of the victim reflecting his/her physical condition and injuries, is obtained. Additional examples of potential evidence may include torn or bloody clothing, medical specimens, and weapons. Remember, evidence should not only be identified, but properly collected as well.

Examples of Evidence:
- A) Clothing *
- B) Specimens *
- C) Weapons
- D) Evidence of assault, i.e., knife blades, bullets.

A) Clothing
- Pack in a paper bag - to air dry (no plastic).
- Check clothing for drugs or weapons etc.
- Maintain chain of custody
- Do not cut through defects on clothing, if possible.
- Do not fold clothing over itself in order to avoid cross - contamination.

B) Specimens
- Obtain the first specimen taken by E.R. personnel

Instruct them not to discard unused specimens.
One week is a reasonable time to maintain medical specimen evidence.
- Ensure test tubes and containers are labeled and dated.
- Maintain chain of custody. The medical facility should have a system and policy approved by the State Attorney or Law Enforcement. A form should be available to assist with the chain of custody.
- Documentation of treatments made due to injuries should be maintained. Documentation of injuries caused by treatments should also be maintained. I.E., I.V. attempts could indicate I.V. drug abuser, therefore all attempts should be documented. All injuries, past and recent, should be documented. Request a body diagram reflecting the injury locations.

PROTECTION/SAFETY PLAN

Obviously, the criminal justice system has failed to protect victims of domestic violence. With this in mind, what can a victim do to protect herself? The development of a safety plan is recommended by Victim Advocate Assistance Programs. In the event you suspect someone is a victim of domestic violence you may recommend the following guidelines in the development of a safety plan.

1) Leave the physical presence of the batterer, if possible.
2) Call 911 or call a local shelter.
3) Scream so your neighbors can hear and will call 911.
4) If you leave by car, lock your doors immediately and do not unlock the doors until you arrive safely at your destination.
5) Check yourself and your children for injuries and go to the hospital if necessary.
6) If you cannot leave, protect yourself to the best of your ability. Survival is a basic human instinct and should not be ignored.

The issue of domestic violence is a serious one. Society must take immediate action to address the problem of domestic violence. Professional investigators must arm themselves with the training and knowledge necessary to properly defeat the ignorance and complacency associated with this tragic problem.

CASE STUDY: DOMESTIC VIOLENCE/2ND DEGREE MURDER

In August of 1990, a 65 year old grandmother, decided to take matters into her own hands. After almost 30 years of verbal and physical abuse by her husband she stabbed her 73 year old husband to death while being attacked in her kitchen. Subsequently, she was arrested and charged with 2nd Degree Murder. The defense launched an aggressive defense based on the theory that the defendant suffered from "Battered Woman Syndrome."

According to witnesses uncovered by private investigators, "the verbal and physical abuse sustained by the defendant was a daily routine." Witnesses provided sworn testimony detailing a regiment of abusive episodes dating as far back as 1962. Injuries sustained by her as a result of the beatings were described as "harsh and severe". Interestingly enough, the witnesses all agreed upon the fact that the defendant's husband was "a kind, easy going man when sober." Unfortunately for his wife, according to witnesses, "he was rarely sober." When the victim was intoxicated witnesses described him as "abusive, violent, intolerable, and just plain mean." A Witness uncovered by defense investigators related that if the defendant killed her husband, "she had no choice - her actions had to be self defense."

The incident on August 25, 1994, resulting in the death of the victim, was not the first time the defendant was forced to defend herself. In 1983, while on a fishing trip, she shot her husband in self defense. According to police reports, the couple was staying in a camper and the victim had been drinking heavily. The defendant went into the camper and retired for the evening. She was later awakened from her sleep when her husband began beating her. The defendant begged him to stop but to no avail. He continued his attack. Desperate to end the brutal attack, the defendant reached into her night dresser, retrieved a .22 caliber handgun, and ordered her husband to "stop or she would shoot!" Unfortunately, he continued his attack and the defendant shot her husband in the stomach. She was arrested and, shortly after, released. The police declared the act as "a clear case of self defense." The victim survived and told police that he loved his wife and did not want to prosecute. He added that "it was all his fault."

Additional acts of violence were also uncovered and documented by defense investigators. Although witnesses provided thorough details of the defendant's beatings at the hands of her husband, the witnesses did not appear to harbor any bad feelings toward him. The consensus among the defense witnesses appeared to be that his violent behavior was caused by his drinking problem. Witnesses described both the victim and the defendant as very kind and caring people, who would go out of their way to help a friend or loved one. "A real tragedy," according to witnesses.

Defense investigators uncovered witnesses who described reports of the defendant being cornered in her room, punched, kicked, and knocked to the floor. She was often beaten severely, having lumps of hair pulled from her head, knocked unconscious with a frying pan, and forced to escape to the homes of neighbors. This was probably the most humiliating for a woman of her background. She was "old fashioned when it came to family," according to witnesses. Witnesses related that she "didn't have the options available to younger women because of her upbringing." It was her belief that she should "stand by her man."

On 6 July 1990, deputies responded to the couple's home in reference to "threats with a knife." Upon arrival, a deputy sheriff related in his report that the victim was "very drunk." According to the arrest affidavit, he told the deputy that "If the two of them (he and his wife) stayed together tonight, he would cut her throat." Although he was arrested, charges against him were not pursued by the state. Approximately a month and a half later, on August 25, 1990, while making lunch for her husband, who was extremely intoxicated, the defendant was again threatened by her husband with a knife. They were in their home. She was preparing lunch at the kitchen counter and he was sitting at the kitchen table drinking. The victim was intoxicated and belligerent. He became very angry and began verbally assaulting his wife. The verbal altercation escalated, resulting in the victim lunging for the defendant's throat. The defendant, who had been cutting tomatoes with a kitchen knife, responded by defending herself with the knife, stabbing her husband of almost 30 years in the chest. The victim fell back into his easy chair and died. Subsequently, the defendant was arrested and charged with 2nd Degree Murder.

Obviously, prosecutors for the State of Florida did not interpret her actions as self defense. Fortunately, for the defendant, her defense attorney did. Under the direction of defense counsel a theory of defense was formed and pursued with fervor. Defense Counsel assembled a defense investigation team led by private investigators. The defense team consisting of the the finest criminal defense investigators and experts in the region began a painstaking investigation into the case. After months of preparation, the case was brought to trial with both the defense and the prosecution presenting compelling cases to the jury. However, the evidence uncovered by the defense investigation and presented by defense counsel was overwhelming. Defense counsel's prosecution of the State's case and cross examination of prosecution witnesses was unyielding. Defense counsel's closing argument was described as "brilliant" as he placed an empty chair in the center of the court room. Defense counsel called upon his final witness, the ghost of the victim, to appear before the court and justify his wife's actions, due to the years of abuse she suffered at his hands.

The trial Judge, jury, and spectators waited in suspense for the ghost of the victim to appear. Defense counsel displayed an intense cross examination of an empty chair allegedly occupied by the ghost of the victim. Defense counsel asked his ghost to tell the jury that his death was not his wife's fault. Just as he told the police when she shot him in self defense in 1983. Based on the juries verdict, it's possible that his ghost did appear before them. It only took the jury 52 minutes to return a verdict and find the defendant "Not Guilty." After the trial, she departed the courtroom with family, friends, and supporters. Her only advice to other victims of domestic violence was "get out early." She died as a result of poor health shortly after being acquitted.

CHAPTER

10

Crime & The Drug War

"

The law is silent during war.

-CICERO

THE ROLE OF THE CRIMINAL DEFENSE INVESTIGATOR

The need for qualified and effective criminal defense investigators has never been greater. The rising tide of violent crime and the never ending drug war has thrown the American criminal justice system into a severe quandary. Crime has literally invaded our society creating a virtual war zone throughout the nation. The inner cities have long been a battle ground in the proclaimed "Drug War". Our cities, under siege and criminal occupation, have become the front lines defending our society in this terrifying war. However, in the past decade, the drug war has spread to suburban and rural America as well. Americans have become witness and often victim to a drastic increase in violent crime as a result of the invasion of illegal drugs into our society. Residents of the inner city have been forced to live on the front lines in this exhausting war with little hope of a cease fire. American cities have literally become combat zones. As the drug war rages on, and the flow of illegal drugs continues to spread and multiply through the streets, it is followed relentlessly by violent crime, a close companion and ally.

Americans have been witness to a steady escalation in the war against drugs over the past decade. Law enforcement and the criminal justice system as a whole have waged a diligent assault against the number one enemy of society known as illegal drugs. Unfortunately, the financial power of the overwhelming opponent is slowly reducing their strength, effectiveness, and morale. The drug war appears to be a no win situation with the objective being containment of the enemy as opposed to victory. America has in the past achieved success in fighting its enemies by rallying the American people, identifying a clearly defined objective, and applying all of its resources to meet the objective. The result, has always been victory. However, America has also entered into various crusades without the support of the people, a clearly defined objective, or commitment of the resources necessary to win. The result, has always been defeat. With this in mind, Americans must make a decision. Either we as a nation defeat this enemy and commit ourselves completely to the cause or we pull out and surrender. Either way, sacrifices have got to be made. Surrender means sacrificing our way of life. The hope of security and safety for our children will be dismal at best. Unopposed, crime will take over our communities and streets as easy as Saddaam Hussain took over Kuwait. Once the enemy becomes rooted, it is much more difficult to remove. Therefore, it would appear that the only plausible option is all out war.

However, keep in mind all out war also comes with a high price. Americans must be willing to make more than just financial sacrifices. In order to support such an effort, Americans must be willing to make personal sacrifices, personal sacrifices such as forgoing basic constitutional rights. In order to effectively combat crime, the American people must be willing to accept suspension of their most precious privileges: the right to bear arms, the right of the people to be secure in their persons, houses, papers, and effects, against unreasonable search and seizures, and the right to due process of law, to name a few. Inevitably, an all out war against drugs, as in all wars, will produce victims of friendly fire. In fact, even limited warfare produces victims of friendly fire.

In modern times, Americans tend to think of war as being fought on foreign soil. However, as we lose ground in the drug war the battlefield is no longer limited to the combat zone. Victims of friendly fire can now be found in suburban and rural areas as well. Such examples have been surfacing all across the nation.

In Morgantown, West Virginia police raided the home of a 72 year old woman, based on what the police claim was a "bad tip". According to a "confidential informant", the suspect residence was cultivating marijuana plants. However, a raid by police was unable to uncover marijuana, finding only 60 pepper and tomato plants.

In Boston, Massachusetts, a drug raid by police left a 75 year old minister dead of a heart attack. The raid was based on information from a paid "confidential informant", rejected two months earlier by police as "unreliable". Prepared and expecting to encounter "four heavily armed drug dealers and a kilogram of cocaine", a SWAT team burst into the apartment of a retired minister. The 75 year old minister described as "frail", was chased into his bedroom by police and handcuffed. The minister collapsed during the struggle and died of heart failure. Police learned that the confidential informant gave the wrong apartment number. The police commissioner later apologized for the incident stating, "The one tragic fact which is clear at this time is that the minister was an innocent victim in the continuing war on drugs."

In Port St. Lucie, Florida a lawsuit filed in U.S. District Court on behalf of an elderly couple, claimed the Port St. Lucie Police Department's Special Response Team or SRT, engaged in a pattern of mistreating and intimidating people and recklessly damaging their property. The law suit alleged that the couple suffered permanent injuries, including the woman having a heart attack, as a result of "improper and unlawful police conduct" by police during a drug raid at their daughter's home. Police claimed that the home, shared by the couple's daughter and two men, was under surveillance for suspected drug activity, and believe that they responded appropriately. "We're not talking about Mr. Roger's Neighborhood, were talking about a crack house," according to the city's attorney. However, the residence in question was an average home, located in an average American neighborhood. Therefore, the City of Port St. Lucie has obviously taken the position that Port St. Lucie neighborhoods are no longer, like Mr. Roger's neighborhood, safe for children. Not unlike cities across the nation, the City of Port St. Lucie appears to be designating its streets a Combat Zone.

On February 2, 1994, the Americans designated to judge the actions of the police, specifically a jury of four men and four women, agreed with the City of Port St. Lucie and exonerated the police department of any wrongdoing. Based on this decision, one can only assume that an all out war against drugs is supported by the people. The decision in this case, as well as jury verdicts across the nation, appears to reflect that Americans support the war on drugs and everything that goes with it, including innocent victims of friendly fire.

The above cases are a perfect example of collateral damage inflicted upon a society during war. The people described were never charged with a crime. They just happened to be in the wrong place at the wrong time: victims of friendly fire.

The war on crime could last longer than any war in our history. In fact, it already has. As the war continues, the casualty rate will increase. As the casualty rate increases the rate of friendly fire victims will increase as well. It is inevitable, that almost everyone will be personally affected, or may even become a victim of friendly fire. America has always fought wars from the moral high ground. The war against drugs appears to be fought from the moral high ground as well. Unquestionably illegal drugs are a menace to our society and should be eliminated. However, the war against drugs, like all wars, should be fought within the rules set forth by a civilized society. In this case, the rules are very clear. The preamble for the rules were written over 200 years ago by our forefathers and documented within the United States Constitution.

"We the people of the United States, in order to form a more perfect Union, establish justice, insure domestic tranquility, provide for the common defense, promote the general welfare, and secure the blessings of liberty to ourselves and our posterity, do ordain and establish this Constitution for the United States of America." These are words to live by.

The American justice system should consider its present course very carefully. The philosophical question of all time is directed at every one of us. Does the end justify the means? The criminal defense investigator is instrumental in determining not only the fate of the innocent victims of friendly fire but the fate of our entire justice system.

This component method is intended to be a guide to assist the criminal defense investigator in the course of his investigation. Utilizing the component method as a reference source for fundamental information, techniques, and skills will enable the criminal defense investigator to perform assigned tasks effectively and efficiently. The component method can be utilized as a preliminary or comprehensive plan. The individual components can be limited or expanded to conform to the specific needs of each case. Proper execution of the component method will allow the criminal defense investigator to submit his final report with the confidence that a thorough investigation was accomplished.

The report of investigation documenting the criminal defense investigator's findings will allow defense counsel to develop a defense strategy based upon facts and not abstract theory. Subsequently, defense counsel may request additional investigation based upon initial findings, investigative recommendations, or supplemental discovery.

This text is intended only as a basic reference guide to be utilized in conjunction with criminal defense investigation assignments. The text may not provide information or guidance to anticipate every situation the criminal defense investigator may encounter in the field. Situations may be encountered that have not been discussed or addressed by this text. If such a situation should arise, the criminal defense investigator should direct all questions to defense counsel prior to engaging in further activity.

REMEMBER, THE BEST DEFENSE IS A STRONG OFFENSE.

Department of the Army, (1985).
Law Enforcement Investigations, FM 19-20.

U.S. Army Military Police School, (1986).
Techniques of Crime Scene Processing, Military Police Investigator's Course.

Richard H. Fox and Carl L. Cunningham, National Institute of Justice, (1988).
Crime Scene Search and Physical Evidence Handbook. Paladin Press.

United States Air Force, (1980).
Security Police Investigator's Guide, AFP 125-2 Volume 1.

United States Air Force, Headquarters Air Force Office of Special Investigations, Directorate of Criminal Investigations, (1977).
Special Investigations Crime Scene Handbook, AFOSIP 124-83.

Brandon A. Perron, Office of the Public Defender, 19th Judicial Circuit, (1994).
Intern Investigator Training Guide.

Office of the Public Defender, 19th Judicial Circuit, (1985).
Student Investigator Manual.

Office of the Public Defender, 15th Judicial Circuit.
Public Defender Investigator's Manual and Office Procedures for Investigators.

F. Lee Bailey & Henry B. Rothblatt, (1985).
Investigation and Preparation of Criminal Cases. Clark, Boardman, Callaghan.

Lenore E. Walker, Ed.D.ABPP, (1993).
Survivor Therapy, Clinical Assessment and Intervention Workbook. Endolor Communications.

J. Michael Aaron, (Nov 1991).
Reflective Ultraviolet Photography Sheds New Light on Pattern Injury. Law & Order Magazine.

Volume 1, Issue IV, (Fall 1994).
The Confidential Informant Crime Magazine.

Volume 2, Issue 1, (Winter 1995).
The Confidential Informant Crime Magazine.

William S. Sahakian & Mabel Lewis Sahakian, (1996)
Ideas of the Great Philosophers, Barnes & Noble Books

Ashton Applewhite, William R. Evans III, & Andrew Frothingham, (1992)
And I Quote, St. Martin's Press

Alibi, Questions, 7-6, 7-7
Witness, 1-3, 8-11
Arrest Affidavit, 8-4, 8-5
Attorney/Client Privilege, Kovel, 4-3, 4-5
Background Investigation, 6-3--6-7
as a component, 1-5, 8-4
sources, 6-3, 6-4
Bail, 4-5
Bailey, F. Lee, quoted, 3-3
Battered Woman Syndrome, 9-3
Blacks Law Dictionary, 1-3
Blackstone, Sr. William, vii
quoted, 1-3
Bond Reduction Form, 4-4
Brouardel, Dr. P.C.H., quoted, 4-7
Chain of Custody, 9-6
Chesterfield, Lord, quoted, 6-2
Cicero, quoted, 10-2
Components, Criminal Defense Investigation,
1-5, 6-3, 8-4--8-18
Component Method, viii, 1-5
Confidentiality, 1-4, 4-3, 4-4
Crime Scene, as a component, 1-5, 8-10
diagram construction, 5-3, 5-7, 5-8
examination of, 5-3--5-16
photograph procedure, 5-5--5-7
Death Penalty, vii
Defendant Interview, 4-3--4-6
as a component, 1-5
in reports, 8-7--8-10
statements, 4-3, 4-4
Dershowitz, Alan, 1-3
Domestic Violence, 9-3
investigative guidelines, 9-4--9-5
Einstein, Albert, quoted, 7-2
Emerson, R.W., quoted, 5-3
Ethics, Criminal Defense Investigator, 1-4
Evidence, classification, 3-6
collection, 9-5, 9-6
documentary, 3-5--3-7
witness, 3-5
Exhibits, in report, 8-17--8-18
Forensic Science, 3-4, 3-7
and truth, 2-3
bloodstain, 5-11--5-12
DNA, 5-14--5-16
fingerprints, 3-5
psychology, 9-3
triangulation, 5-8
Franklin, Benjamin, quoted, 4-23
Giuardoux, Jean, quoted, 2-2
Grego, Richard, M.A., D.A., v
Hanks, Nancy, quoted, 8-2
Investigations, Criminal Defense,
1-3, 1-4, 6-3, 10-3--10-4
Investigative Case Review, 3-3--3-9
as a component, 1-5
example, 8-7
Investigative Journal, 3-8, 3-9
Investigative Outline, 3-7--3-8
Kennedy-Smith, William, 4-5
911 Records, in report, 8-13
Pasteur, Louis, quoted, 3-2
Perron, Brad A., Criminalist,
Forensic Consultant, 5-11
Perron, Brandon A., v
Philosophy, for Criminal Defense
Investigators, 2-3--2-5
Photographs, in Investigative Reports, 5-5--5-7
Plea-bargain, 4-5
Polygraph, 4-3--4-5
Post-Traumatic Stress Disorder, 9-3
Protagorus, 3-1
Public Defender, 8-4
Reasonable Doubt, defined, 1-3
in Criminal Defense Investigations, 1-3, 3-3
Report of Investigation, 1-4, 8-3, 8-4
as a component, 1-5
example of, 8-4--8-18
Shaw, George Bernard, quoted, 9-2
Simpson, O.J., 9-3
Summary of Investigation, example, 8-15--8-17
Sworn Statements, 1-4
recording of, 7-4
Timeline, 3-5--3-6
in report, 8-14--8-15
Truth, vii, 2-3--2-5, 4-5
absolute/relative, 2-5
standards of, 2-3--2-4
Twain, mark, quoted, 8-2
Voice-Stress Analysis, 4-5
Witness Interview, 1-4, 3-4--3-7, 7-3--7-4
example of 8-11--8-12
as a component, 1-5
questions for, 7-5--7-7

INDEX OF CASE STUDIES

Background Investigation, 4-6, 6-4--6-5
Bloodstain, 5-13--5-14, 6-6
Bond, 5-13, 6-4
Burglary, Dwelling, 5-8
Crime Scene, 5-8, 5-10, 5-12
Defendant Interview, 4-6
Domestic Violence, 9-6--9-8
Evidence, Documentary, 3-7
Physical, 5-10, 5-13
Witness, 4-5, 6-6, 7-8
Homicide/Murder, 3-7, 5-10, 5-12, 6-5, 9-6
Investigative Case Review, 3-7
Luminol Test, 5-10
Polygraph, 4-6
Report of Investigation, 3-7
Self-Defense, 9-7
Sworn Statement, 7-8
Witness Interview, 3-7, 5-8, 7-7